BEYOND EVEREST

*One Sherpa's Summit
and Hope for Nepal*

By
Corinne Richardson
With Pem Dorjee Sherpa

Printed in the United States of America

Hardcover ISBN: 978-1-961624-84-9
Paperback ISBN: 978-1-961624-85-6
Ebook ISBN: 978-1-961624-86-3
Library of Congress Control Number: 2024910604

DartFrog Plus is the hybrid publishing imprint of DartFrog Books, LLC.

301 S. McDowell St.
Suite 125-1625
Charlotte, NC 28204
www.DartFrogBooks.com

Publisher's Cataloging-in-Publication
(Provided by Cassidy Cataloguing Services, Inc.).

Names: Richardson, Corinne M., author. | Sherpa, Pem Dorjee, author.
Title: Beyond Everest : one Sherpa's summit and hope for Nepal / by Corinne Richardson ; with Pem Dorjee Sherpa.
Description: Charlotte, NC : DartFrog Books, [2024] | Includes bibliographical references.
Identifiers: ISBN: 978-1-961624-84-9 (hardcover) | 978-1-961624-85-6 (paperback) | 978-1-961624-86-3 (ebook) | 978-1-961624-87-0 (audiobook) | LCCN: 2024910604
Subjects: LCSH: Sherpa, Pem Dorjee. | Mulepati, Moni. | Sherpa (Nepalese people)--Biography. | Newar (Nepalese people)--Biography. | Sherpa (Nepalese people)--Social life and customs. | Newar (Nepalese people)--Social life and customs. | Mountaineers--Nepal--Biography. | Everest, Mount (China and Nepal)--Personal narratives. | Adventure and adventurers--Everest, Mount (China and Nepal) | Survival--Everest, Mount (China and Nepal) | Intermarriage-Nepal. | Caste--Nepal. | Himalaya Mountains--Economic conditions. | Nepal--Politics and government--21st century. | Sherpa (Nepalese people)--United States. | Immigrants--United States--Biography. | LCGFT: Personal narratives. | Autobiographies. | True adventure stories. | BISAC: BIOGRAPHY & AUTOBIOGRAPHY / Adventurers & Explorers. | BIOGRAPHY & AUTOBIOGRAPHY / Survival. | BIOGRAPHY & AUTOBIOGRAPHY / Asian & Asian American. | SPORTS & RECREATION / Mountaineering. | TRAVEL / Asia / Central.
Classification: LCC: DS493.9.S5 R53 2024 | DDC: 954.96--dc23

And here I am, you say, here, still, I am.
—Joyce Carol Oates,
"Undertow, Wolf's Head Lake"

ADVANCE PRAISE

"Richardson's uplifting debut recounts Pem Dorjee Sherpa's story—his life, love, success, and eventual immigration to the United States. Her description of Pem's harsh childhood, the poverty, and lack of opportunities is both sensitive and authentic; by placing those experiences in the broader cultural, economic, and social conditions of Nepal, she gives them context and breadth. This is a crisp, inspiring account not just of scaling a deadly summit, but of life itself."

— BookLife Review

"*Beyond Everest* is not just an adventure story, but one that's grounded in love, partnership, and a shared vision. Richardson is a trustworthy narrator who reveals a nuanced understanding of Pem and Moni's challenges and secrets, and invites readers into the ascendancy that results when we devote ourselves to each other and our communities."

— Sonya Lea,
author of the memoir, *Wondering Who You Are*

"This is no ordinary climbing story. With all the drama, ambition and adventure of a good mountaineering read—including descriptions so vivid you feel the experience viscerally— the stakes here reach far beyond survival and summits. Richardson's spare, graceful prose captures Pem Sherpa's humble voice, rooted in, yet struggling against, the culture and realities of his homeland. A moving, rare window into an unexpected and deeply felt journey, to create a life shaped by love for both mountains and family.

— Susan Futrell,
author, *Good Apples: Behind Every Bite*

"As a Sherpa mountaineer, I can relate to Pem Dorjee Sherpa's story told in *Beyond Everest*, and Moni's too. It is very difficult for Sherpa climbers, especially women climbers to get sponsorships and recognition for our skills and contributions to climbing. Beyond Everest is an encouraging story—a must read."

— Lhakpa Sherpa, 10-time Everest summiter, the most of any woman in the world. Summited K2 July 27, 2023. Stars in documentary film, *Mountain Queen*

"For hundreds of years Sherpas did the hard work for Himalaya expeditions. Now, they are leading tourists up to the highest summits and being recognized for their mountaineering skills as we see with Pem Dorjee Sherpa's story in *Beyond Everest*."

— Reinhold Messner, acclaimed mountaineer, author of *Everest: Expedition to the Ultimate*, *The Crystal Horizon: Everest, the First Solo Ascent*, *My Life at the Limit*

"I was hooked on this book from the first pages. Corinne Richardson's writing about a remarkable Sherpa and his

Newari climbing partner is poetic, evocative, and riveting. I routinely found myself reading passages aloud to anyone within earshot—something I rarely do. It's a story that left me changed; one that I won't soon forget."

— Megan Regnerus, writer, editor. Editor Emeritus, *Montana Quarterly*. Her writing has appeared in magazines including *Montana Quarterly, Runner's World, Tributary, Outside Bozeman, Brain Child, Aegist,* and *Next Avenue*

"Pem Dorjee Sherpa's journey is nothing short of extraordinary. *Beyond Everest* offers a gripping and heartfelt account of a man who faced death on the world's highest peak and overcame unimaginable challenges to rise above his circumstances. His story of resilience, courage, and hope will inspire anyone who reads it."

— Sean Swarner, author of *Keep Climbing: How I Beat Cancer and Reached the Top of the World*

"Moni's accomplishments as a Newari woman were extraordinary. What she risked for love is heroic. A beautiful story."

— Maya Sherpa, President, Everest Summiters Association, Nepal. Seven-time 8000m summiter and first Nepali woman to summit Ama Dablam, Pumori, Cho Oyu, Baruntse, Khan Tengri, and Himlung

"With rich and lyrical prose, *Beyond Everest* takes us into the heart of Everest, immersing us in the world of a Nepali family struggling for survival, showing beauty and violence, poverty and resilience, and love and desperation. Deeply felt and bursting with beautiful imagery and dramatic scenes, this book would make a stunning movie."

— Jack Horner, American Paleontologist, Presidential Fellow, Chapman University

"I am thrilled to see more Sherpa experiences being shared with the world. Pem's courageous story highlights many aspects of our beautiful culture and way of life in small villages, as well as the challenges we face. Pem has confronted one of the greatest challenges of all: climbing Everest. Through this remarkable achievement, he has found a way to support his family and village while giving back to Nepal. What an incredible accomplishment!"

— AC Sherpa, President and Founder of 7 Summits Foundation, Honorary Consul General, Government of Nepal to Washington State, US

"This book is a must read for travelers to Nepal. The author chronicles the life of Pem Dorjee Sherpa and provides a compelling portrait of Sherpa village life. The pages draw the reader into colorful descriptions of the mountain landscapes of eastern Nepal and explore the complex emotional landscape faced when emigrating from one's home country as seen through the heart of Pem Sherpa."

— Mary Hubbard, PhD, Retired Professor, Montana State University, Fulbright Scholar grant recipient to Nepal for collaborative research on Himalayan fault zones, and author of *Geological Field Excursion Guidebook of Malekhu Area, Central Nepal Himalaya*

"The story of Moni Mulepati and Pem Sherpa is truly inspiring and heartwarming. Their love and bravery shine through as they secretly marry at the summit of Everest. Their journey shows their determination to conquer both the mountain and Nepal's societal expectations, with their love adding a beautiful layer of emotion to their amazing story. It was an honor for me to be part of the expedition as a team member and spontaneous Groomsman!"

— Kami Sherpa, Nepali mountaineer, photographer, and news reporter. Six-time Everest summiteer and the first TV journalist to broadcast live news from the summit of Mt Everest

"Pem Dorjee Sherpa's moving life story reveals the essence of a Sherpa's life – struggles, ambition, commitment, love and resilience. However, his story is beyond that of a dedicated, hard-working Sherpa; it's a human story of survival, ingenuity and hope. Struggling to find his place in life, Pem's story can inspire everyone to live their life to their fullest potential."

— Alan Arnette, Everest summiteer, blogger, climbing coach

"Poignant and heartfelt, Richardson delivers a stunning narrative in this true story of a Nepalese climbing Sherpa – a tale of extreme poverty and childhood abuse, the challenges of Mt Everest and the possibility of forbidden love. Written with gripping details and masterful clarity."

— Thomas Elliott, speaker, writer, publisher. His short stories, essays, and poetry have been featured in *The New Montana Story, High Plains News, On Flat Willow Creek, a History of Montana's N-Bar Ranch, Desert Rain House: Resilient Building, Sustainable Living in the High Desert*

"A beautifully inspiring book filled with hardship, inspiration and triumph! Reading the words on the pages increased my desire to return as I so enjoy the beauty of the Everest region and the kind people who live there. I can almost taste the foods, feel the atmosphere as I experience again, through the descriptive writing, the valued jewels the people of Nepal are. Pem and Moni's life story is a banner of hope in our challenging world, and shows the courage it takes to reach one's dreams."

— Gerri Kier,
Founder, Education Elevated

"In the true story, *Beyond Everest*, Corinne Richardson takes us on the fantastic journey of Pem Dorjee Sherpa's life story. Raised in a mystical, remote village in the high Himalayas, the young runaway flees a life of subsistence farming, poverty and hardship. A serendipitous romance and adventure whisk him to the icy slopes of Mount Everest where he and his girlfriend shatter pervasive cultural norms. Hard-won, Pem's life is a life most villagers will never know."

— Heather O'Neal,
Founder, Of Global Interest Adventure Travel Company

"As the first Newari woman to summit Mount Everest, Moni's accomplishments were groundbreaking. In *Beyond Everest*, her story and courageous decision to risk everything for love is truly inspiring."

— Pasang Lhamu Sherpa, Climbing Instructor, 2016 National Geographic Adventurer of the Year, and first Nepali woman to summit K2

"For many of us in Nepal, Pem Dorjee Sherpa is a hero. He and Moni's contributions to Chyangba village and to many Nepali children who have received an education, show his dedication to Nepal. A true testament to the realities of poverty in rural villages."

— Ang Phula Sherpa, Everest Mountaineer and Actor in David Breashears' feature film, *Everest* (2015)

"This book is a must read for anyone who's interested in powerful stories of success."

— Greg S. Reid, speaker, filmmaker, and author of *Three Feet from Gold*, *The Secret of Happiness, and Footsteps of the Fearless*

CONTENTS

A FEW WORDS
TO THE READER

Namaste. My given name is PemDorjee Sherpa. I was born and raised in Chyangba, a small village in Nepal. I think I was born in 1982, but I'm not totally sure. We don't keep good birth records in my village. Many years later, when I got my first passport, my name was written as Pem Dorjee Sherpa, and that's what I go by now. I'm often confused with Sherpas named Pemba Sherpa. Sherpa kids are usually named for the day of the week they are born. Kids born on Saturday are called Pemba, but the monk who was in the village the day I was born named me Pem.

My childhood life was simple but hard. There were no roads, electricity, or running water in my village. We were subsistence farmers and worked in our fields near our home. My dad and mom worked hard to raise six children, but sometimes we didn't have enough food to eat. Many Sherpas have similar stories of hard work and sacrifice, but not many Sherpa stories get told. My story is a bit unique because I was able to overcome the hardship my family was facing and help educate my siblings. Unfortunately, most Sherpas are unable to change their situation because of a lack of education and good-paying jobs in Nepal.

I was fortunate to be able to leave Nepal, and thanks to the help of many friends, my wife and I are now US citizens. Immigrating to the US was a mix of emotions. I was scared and missed Nepal, but me and my wife are an intercaste marriage, and it was hard for us to get along with our family and community. Also, we didn't have a good financial situation in Nepal, so we felt relief and hope with more opportunities in the US.

I couldn't write this book myself because my English is not good and I'm not a writer. Sherpas don't read much and many, like my parents, don't know how to write. In Sherpa, the language my family and I speak, we don't use a lot of words to describe things, and sometimes it's hard to find a word in English that has the same meaning. Also, in Nepal, we don't talk much about our childhood the way Americans do. Many times, when I asked my parents to explain something about our family history or traditions, they thought the questions were really strange and laughed at me. They are proud of my work and everything I have done, but they don't understand about writing stories for the public. Even if I could write a book, I think it would be impossible now because my wife and I are raising our two girls and running several businesses to support our families.

I am so lucky to meet Corinne Richardson, who is willing to give her time and energy to share my stories with the world. I found Corinne through my good friend, Mary Grace Wilkus, who lives in Wyoming and Montana. Mary Grace has generously supported many projects in Chyangba Village. She has also helped hundreds of underprivileged Nepali girls get an education and have more opportunities than their parents had. I am very grateful to Mary Grace for her passion for Nepali people and for introducing me to Corinne.

I chose Corinne to write my story because she understood and cared about telling it truthfully. She traveled to my home village, to Everest Basecamp, and to Kathmandu many times with me to learn more about my story and lifestyle. She often stayed with me and my family as we worked on the book, and I stayed at her home in Montana. Because of these connections with Corinne, sharing my stories with her felt really comfortable for me, and she became like family.

Even my oldest daughter, Pelzom, got involved with the book, helping to translate and find the right words to express Sherpa and Newari culture the way Moni and I experienced it. At home, Moni and I decided to speak only Nepali to our girls so they would be bilingual and know something about Sherpa and Newari culture. We take our girls back to Nepal whenever we can, so they will get to know our families and traditions.

My greatest hope for my daughters is that they have the opportunity to follow their dreams and live a better life than what I had growing up in Nepal. I think education is most important, so I am working hard to educate both girls so they don't have to face the challenges I had when I was growing up.

I know many other Sherpas with interesting life stories who are unable to share them with the world because of a lack of education and opportunity. I hope this book will help other Sherpas find a way to get their stories published and share more about our Nepali culture. And most of all, I hope the future brings more opportunities to people in Nepal.

—Pem Dorjee Sherpa

MAPS

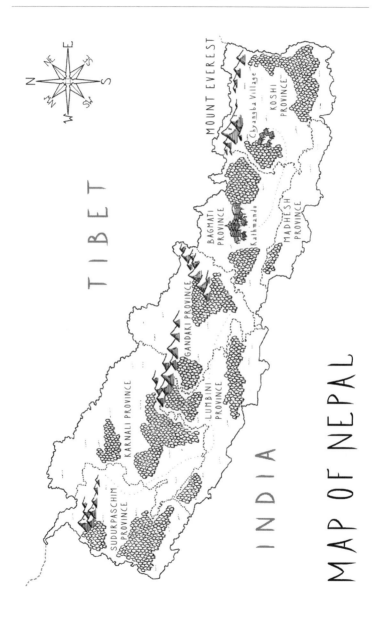

MAP OF NEPAL

PROLOGUE

In the Sherpa Cultural Museum above Namche Bazaar Nepal, there is a room filled with portraits of every Sherpa who has summited Mt. Everest. Rows and rows of Sherpa faces are tacked to wood walls, waist high to the rafters, each containing a brief bio below their name. The climbers are predominantly men, with a few Sherpa women here and there, mostly on the recent wall. The collection begins in the 1950s and includes a famous photograph of Tenzing Norgay Sherpa assigning loads to porters during the 1953 British expedition with Sir Edmund Hillary, the first confirmed climbers to have reached Everest's summit, and another of Tenzing posing with legendary climbers like Tibetan Sherpa Nawang Gombu, the first man in the world to climb Everest twice. The backgrounds vary in each photograph. In some, the mountaineers stand on the summit, their bright summit suits zipped high to their chins, ice clinging to their face, a fierce wind blowing sideways. Other photos depict Sherpas at a Solokhumbu teahouse, a village backyard, a business office, a monastery. Some smile wildly, beaming with joy, while others scowl or squint into the searing Himalayan sun, their clothing and gear reflecting a specific climbing era.

As I look at each Sherpa face, I wonder what these climbers confronted on their journeys. *Late Ang Dorjee Sherpa. Late*

Sungdare Sherpa. How did they die? Old age, an accident on Everest, a fatal health condition that crept in unexpectedly? Sungdare, I would learn, summited Everest five times, and on more than one expedition had witnessed multiple deaths in harrowing conditions. In 1979, it is reported, that while climbing with a German team, exhausted and out of oxygen, unable to descend, he and two team members spent the night in a snow cave in the Death Zone just below the summit. Worried that his two team members would die without oxygen, Sungdare, in bad shape himself, climbed to a lower camp, retrieved an oxygen tank he had stashed for the descent, and climbed back up. When he returned, one climber was dead, the other fading. In the end, oxygen and heroic efforts were not enough to save the two climbers. Sungdare, frostbitten and barely able to walk, his vision impaired from snow blindness, stumbled his way to lower elevation where climbers helped him down to Basecamp, then to a Kathmandu hospital. Though he survived the ordeal and continued to climb for a living, Sungdare succumbed to alcoholism and died by suicide in 1989, becoming another haunting casualty of Everest and austere living conditions in Nepal.

The portraits with longer bios reflect world-record holding achievements.

Lhakpa Gyalu Sherpa: summited Mt. Everest in 10 hours 56 minutes.

Apa Sherpa: first to climb Everest 21 times.

Kami Rita Sherpa: first to climb Everest 25 times.

Near the end of the hall, up near the ceiling, between Zamling Tenzing Sherpa and Tul Sing Gurung, I find the photo I've been searching for:

Pem Dorjee Sherpa. Chyangba, Tapting, Solukhumbu 30th May 2005 Rotary Expedition South Col. He climbed with his girlfriend Moni Mulepati and married on the summit.

In the photograph, Pem Sherpa is wearing a bright yellow athletic jacket zipped to his chin. His young, moon-shaped face looks straight ahead, lips slightly parted as if beginning a smile or blurting one last word before the camera shutter snapped. He looks surprised. His shiny black hair falls in a jagged line across his forehead as though trimmed hastily with dull kitchen shears. His bangs float off his forehead casting a shadow over his eyebrows.

I hiked up to the museum on a cool October morning just as the staggering snowcapped Himalayas emerged from a wall of clouds that had settled in the jet stream a few days earlier, cutting the mountains out of the landscape. I hiked slowly, my breath catching in the altitude, and stopped to rest on a tight, steep switchback. Namche was just waking up. Furry brown and white yaks carrying bulky loads wove along the dusty paths, yak bells clanging up and down the mountain as their owners whistled them on. Villagers bustled around yards organizing the supplies they had spread out into individual loads to be carried up the mountain. As I labored to breathe, men of all ages, and boys too, hoisted baskets with massive loads onto their backs—gas tanks, oxygen cylinders, steel beams, jugs of water, enormous bags of rice, cooking and camping gear, hundreds of duffel bags stuffed with trekkers' belongings. Some Sherpas struggled to lift the *doko*, the woven bamboo basket, onto their backs solo, while others enlisted the help of nearby humans. Stunned by the weight these Sherpas carry and my own difficulty breathing, I couldn't imagine climbing nearly three times higher to 29,000 feet.

Everest, it seems to me, is one of those places where you question the rightness of things—the difficulty, the how and why of it all, a climb through a deadly, moving icefall, and the Death Zone, the oxygen deprived area above 26,247 feet where nightmarish things happen to the body and many climbers die. It was a challenge to make sense of the ethical debates about the outsourcing of risk to Sherpas and the environmental and cultural impacts on the Everest region, and the ways in which death, in the world of extreme climbing, is viewed as a normal part of life, with climbers stepping over dying mountaineers on their way to or from the summit and refusing to help.

As these thoughts swirled in my head, I watched a young boy who looked about thirteen settle a load on his shoulders and start up the mountain. My mind turned back to Pem Sherpa. I tried to imagine him working these paths, a twelve-year-old porter weighing all of eighty pounds, a massive load hanging from his slight frame.

I first met Pem Dorjee Sherpa in Big Sky, Montana in 2016. It was a crisp autumn day, the time of year when snow tips the high peaks, elk bugle in the meadows and forests, and mountain light pales early and darkness comes quick. He was speaking at a fundraising event dedicated to educating Nepali girls, many of whom were orphans, some from his own village in Chyangba.

Back then, what I knew about Pem Dorjee Sherpa was that he had summited Everest, that he was raised in a remote village in Nepal in a family of subsistence farmers, and that his third world existence had sometimes put his life in jeopardy. As Pem spoke, guests crowded around him, drawn into the stories shared by this young, black-haired, soft-spoken Buddhist Sherpa from a Nepal village no one had ever heard of. Pem spoke of harrowing life events with surprising calm and matter-of-factness, with smiles and humor, and seemingly little evidence of pain or sorrow. Like everyone else in the room, I was immediately moved by his stories. *How did he escape from the village? What were the other stories?* I wondered.

I have always had an interest in survival stories—reversals of apocalyptic situations and the determination to survive; in what we are willing or not willing to sacrifice for ourselves or someone else to save ourselves or others. I had read a fair amount of epic rescue and survival stories and tragedies on Everest, in the woods, and at sea. Sebastian Junger's book, *The Perfect Storm,* was a story that hit home. My father knew and fished with the crew aboard the *Andrea Gail* that sank off the coast of Massachusetts in 1991 in one of the most catastrophic storms in history.

My interest in Pem Sherpa's life story probably has something to do with my own upbringing. Although our backgrounds are extremely different—culturally, educationally, and to some degree, economically—there were surprising similarities about our childhood circumstances that made me consider things in a new and interesting way. Like Pem, I understood what it meant to live in poverty, living off the land in an isolated geographical area, and I knew the cruel hands and lips of an alcoholic parent. Most of our food came from the woods, the sea, and what we raised—venison, fish, chicken, pigs, garden vegetables. When the fishing season was inadequate to support our family of seven, we relied on food stamps for the basics: milk, cereal, bread. But unlike Pem and his family, we always had food. Even when sparse, we could fall back on a handout from church or a family member. We lived in an affluent country where there was at least the possibility of economic assistance, medical care, and opportunities, albeit with glaring inequalities.

I knew the dangerous, Russian roulette-like dance that comes with working in an unforgiving landscape. In Pem's descriptions of Everest, I heard echoes of the fierce environment of my childhood, the Atlantic Ocean and Gulf of Maine where my family has made a living fishing commercially for five generations. In our small island community, men and women live and die in the orbital progression of weather, waves, wind, and current—how the Labrador Current collides with the Gulf Stream, and the way life comes. Most days, we didn't know if the people we loved and depended on would return home. The Atlantic, while not host to the extreme altitudes of Everest, has equally awesome and capricious power and possesses its own version of a Death Zone where even an experienced fisherman's life can be taken in an instant.

I knew the anxious worry that gripped Sherpa families when their loved ones left for Everest, gone for weeks and months at a time with limited means of communication. Every time my father, and later my brothers, went to sea, our entire family worried. Sometimes Dad was back in a day, but when he set out for the Georges Bank fishing grounds 200 miles from home, navigating through dangerous crosscurrents and fog, he was gone a week or more. When I was eight years old, on a cold February night in a frothy winter sea, my father's boat engine suddenly quit and radio communication with him was lost. His trawler, coated in ice and frozen sea spray, drifted in the tidal current until it caught and ripped open on the rocks. Brutally frigid air tugged at the wool pants and oilskins my father wore, a salt mist seeped into his lungs. As his fishing boat sank, my father plunged into the turbulent, icy Atlantic, drunk and alone in pitch-black darkness. His expected survival time in the thirty-three-degree sea was less than fifteen minutes. The following day, the US Coast Guard rescued him from a small island a half mile from where his boat sank, twenty-five miles from home. He had walked all night and half a day to stay conscious and beat hypothermia.

The fallout of accidents and miscalculations that happen in remote places like Everest, the Atlantic Ocean, or an isolated Maine island, can cut holes in a family and community. Pem knows many of the orphaned children who lost parents on Everest and were sent to work to support the family, or worse, sold to labor camps or the sex trade. The Sherpa Four, for instance, four siblings who had lost their entire family in the 2015 earthquake, were discovered performing hard labor along the Everest route, their bodies rawboned and their hair full of lice. Then there was Sachan, a young boy whose father died while carrying climbers' gear to Everest. His father had taken the higher paying job so he could send his children to school, only to leave them orphaned and his wife in poverty.

I understand these losses, too. In the Maine woods, while bird hunting, my grandfather tripped over a log and shot his arm off. He was eighteen. Alone, in shock and bleeding heavily, his wrist dangling by a thread of skin, he walked home. Medical care was hours away by ferry to the mainland, followed by a forty-minute drive to the hospital. My grandfather survived and learned to lobster fish and herring seine with one arm, but his accident forever changed the economic and emotional dynamics of our family. The generational violence would repeat itself in 1979. Like my grandfather, I also survived an accidental shooting in the Maine woods while hunting. I was eighteen. I did not lose a limb, but the fallout was harsh. I dropped out of college and lost my bearings for the better part of a decade.

A year after our first meeting, Pem and I met up again in Big Sky at a TEDx talk where he was a guest speaker on the topic of surmounting challenges. As we talked, Pem opened up more about personal details of his life. The childhood he endured, what he had to overcome, and his harrowing experiences at Everest were wildly shocking to me. I was fascinated by his Sherpa village life and culture. In all the books I had read about Everest, I couldn't recall many Sherpa narratives except for books about Tenzing Norgay. I told Pem that I'd like to help write his story, although I expected him to say no, preferring an established or best-selling writer like Jon Krakauer, author of *Into Thin Air*, with whom Pem had crossed paths during an expedition.

We spent some time talking about the fact that there are very few Sherpa stories in the vast cannon of Everest climbing literature.

"I think maybe because we don't have the language skills," Pem speculated. "We don't know how to write books and there's no access to publishing." Generally speaking, Nepalis don't read much, especially in remote villages where education is limited or absent, he added. "We watch movies, but only in theaters."

In the villages, owning or having access to a TV is rare. At the end of our conversation, Pem agreed to collaborate on a book about his experiences, but first, we both acknowledged that I had to climb to Everest Basecamp and up to the Khumbu Icefall with him.

Our journey began in 2017 with the forty-minute flight from Kathmandu to Lukla, the starting point for most trekkers and climbers. Flying into the busy Tenzing-Hillary Airport is a hair-raising experience. It was a clear day, but the airport is often shrouded in fog, leaving passengers stranded for hours, sometimes days. As we approached the single runway, the plane suddenly dropped, and a loud bang released from the plane. The runway shortened in lightning speed. As the plane whizzed past trees, stone lodges, prayer flags, and a wire fence, heading straight toward the mountain, I gasped. The landing gear slammed the pavement, pitching passengers forward into the seat ahead, and bumped along the broken white line in the runway, its nose lurching side to side. The plane taxied toward the tower, made an S turn to set up for takeoff, and jolted to a stop.

The Tenzing-Hillary Airport is one of the most treacherous runways in the world. At about 9,000 feet, the short, paved runway is surrounded by mountains and a sheer cliff with a 2,000-foot drop directly below. At this altitude, low air density reduces lift, and lower air resistance makes it harder to slow a plane down. Add the problem of a short runway for takeoff and landing—a mere 1,729 feet compared to a commercial runway of 8,000 to 13,000 feet—plus frequently deteriorating weather conditions, and it's a recipe for disaster. In the Himalaya, clouds are persistent and can close in quickly, turning into a dense fog that obscures all visibility. There are no "go arounds" at the Lukla airport. The approach is final. Pilots must land on the first try or perish in a fiery crash in the trees below or the mountain above. Although the Nepali government sets high training standards for pilots flying into Lukla, still, the airport has an accident-ridden history.

Pem and I spent fourteen days trekking to Everest Basecamp and back, acclimatizing along the way. In Gorak Shep, at 16,942 feet, the last lodging before the tent city of Everest Basecamp, it was difficult to breathe, sleep, and eat. I settled into my room, a sparse closet-like space with squeaky wood floors, two small bed frames topped with a thin mattress pad, and one small lamp stand. This is not a place you could get used to. That evening, in the adjacent room, an eleven-year-old boy screamed relentlessly while his parents, two doctors on a family trip to Everest Basecamp, tried to soothe him. He had developed high altitude sickness, which can make your head feel like it's exploding. The Diamox altitude sickness medication his parents administered brought no relief to the boy. They had no choice but to descend and had arranged for a helicopter to fly them to a Kathmandu hospital the next day, hoping he would make it through the night.

For acute mountain sickness, the only cure is descent, but a full recovery, or that you will even make it down, is never a guarantee. Pem has seen climbers and trekkers placed inside a Gamow Bag, a hyperbaric chamber, which, when inflated, increases the concentration of oxygen molecules, simulating a descent. In ten minutes, one could simulate descending 7,000 feet. The effect can last twelve hours, and in a best-case scenario, long enough to get down on your own power. But usually, there's no turning back for a second shot at Everest.

After reaching Basecamp, we hiked another hour up to the Khumbu Icefall at the foot of the Western Cwm (pronounced 'coom') where an entry permit from the Nepali government is required. From a pile of rock and scree, I scanned the miles of massive ice seracs and hanging glaciers stretching up toward the Lhotse face and the rocky spur of Nuptse off to our right expecting to see Mt. Everest, but the mountain was hidden behind Lhotse. From the South side, unless you climb Kala Patthar on the ridge of Pumori just above Gorak Shep, the first glimpse of Everest doesn't appear until you've climbed through the Icefall and up the Western Cwm towards Camps I and II. Pem pointed out the general route he had taken through the Icefall in 2005. The route changes every year as the landscape shifts with avalanches and falling seracs. Sometimes, mid-season, after a devastating avalanche, Sherpas have to set a new course. While Pem was talking, the earth cracked and groaned and trembled beneath our feet, like it might split open any second.

"It's so noisy, it's difficult to sleep here," Pem said. "The ground is moving and it's hard to find flat spot to set up a tent," he added, kicking at rocks and ice in the frozen, sloped ground.

After ending our Basecamp trek back in Namche, we flew by helicopter to Chyangba and stayed with Pem's family. When we arrived, the whole clan and half the village greeted us. For villagers, it was rare and spectacular to see a helicopter land in Chyangba, and Pem was treated like a dignitary, a local hero.

When I arrived back home in Montana and reflected on the experience, I had a deep belief that this book had to be written. To be immersed in the landscape and culture of Everest with Pem and his family, and to see and hear directly of the adversity he and others had to overcome, was incredibly powerful. In Michigan a year later, when I met Pem's wife, Moni Mulepati, for the first time, she said something that I would never forget:

> *Sherpas are like God at Everest. They give you their life. They give their full energy to help you, but they cannot do everything. You have to climb. Without Sherpas, no one would summit Everest.*

Tearing up as she looked me in the eye, her words, and the emotion behind them, felt like a deep recognition. Like honor. At the time, I was a stranger to her, and the honesty and poignancy of her words affirmed my conviction that this story belongs in the world. To me, the absence of many generations of these culturally rich Sherpa narratives feels like a huge void.

This book is the result of years of collaboration with Pem and many trips to Nepal together, with visits to his family home in Chyangba and Michigan and to Moni's family in Kathmandu. I had the honor of being the writer and collaborator with Pem as we teased out segments of his story, a story that intersects many cultures. While the book mainly portrays the life story of Pem Dorjee Sherpa and his wife, Moni Mulepati, it is also, in part, a shared story of many Nepalese climbing Sherpas, their families, villages, the fabric of their lives and culture, their struggles, spiritual journeys, hopes, and possibilities. As I have learned through Pem and the incredible people I have met in Nepal, there are many powerful, engaging Sherpa stories that remain to be told.

PART I

आत्मा ATMA
SPIRIT OF A SHERPA

Mother Nature tries to kill them every autumn and spring after the monsoons clear out and the weather turns. Still, Nepali Sherpas slog up the Solukhumbu Valley toward Everest on foot, exceedingly heavy loads lashed to their backs. They trek through farms and villages, past monasteries, prayer wheels and sacred shrines, passing *mani* stones inscribed with mantras, and stone memorials of Everest's dead, each pile of stones draped with prayer flags. They trek through gorgeous vistas that Everest-bound clients would die for. For days, weeks, months, in pummeling snow and raging wind, in minus fifty-degree temperatures and blistering sun, they move equipment, supplies, gear and climbers to Sagarmatha's summit. Sagarmatha, the Nepali name for Everest, means sky, *sagar*, and head, *matha*, so something like: forehead touching the sky.

The Sherpas cross mountains and valleys, ancient trade routes, and the wildly treacherous Khumbu Icefall. Alone or with yaks, they walk and walk and haul loads through their ancestral hills, through avalanche debris and piles of weather-beaten climbing ropes and trash. They walk over dead bodies. Bodies perfectly preserved in ice. Bodies partially or totally exposed lying face up, face down, sitting on a slope, near a ladder, at the edge of a crevasse, in a crevasse, at a common rest spot along the route. In some odd, random place where a climber suddenly dropped, an ice-crusted hand appears, a leg, a skull bulging from the icy mountain. A patch of hair waving in the wind. They are the bodies of western climbers and of Sherpas—a Sherpa porter who lugged gear, cooked, cleaned, and broke trail so westerners could summit; a Sherpa climber, a guide, a cook, an Icefall Doctor who fixed ropes and ladders—all of them someone's father, brother, son, daughter, a husband, a family provider. These dead bodies collapse into Everest's landscape becoming landmarks of sorts, marking the distance to the summit, warning of a danger ahead or in the past—each abandoned, iced-over body an uncomfortable reminder of mortality and the toll of climbing the world's tallest mountain.

High up in the shadows of Everest, while Sherpas are in a tented sleep, clouds edge silently and powerfully in and out of the Himalayas, gathering into a killer storm or dispersing with mercy. All day, all night, the earth beneath and above them shudders, shifts, and breaks, sending rubble thundering down a near mountainside. They work and sleep to the sounds of a war zone. Each dawn, the day pries open with looming possibilities of death. Sherpas pray. They pray to Sagarmatha for permission to summit. *Everest, sacred mountain, forgive us for walking on you.* They pray for life. For protection. They pray to be saved from whatever trouble lies ahead because they know that in the lap of Everest, trouble routinely comes, closes in swiftly as a surging wave and chokes. They pray for the physical and mental fortitude to climb because their livelihoods and families depend upon it. Prayers are offered for mothers and sisters and brothers and children waiting at home in villages, and for fathers, too, if they are still alive, yet unclaimed by Everest. Some Sherpas pray as the numbing effects of alcohol wear off after a night of drinking to soothe nerves and dull the dread of climbing through the Icefall and Death Zone. These prayers are not just a Sherpa tradition, but a safety line—a fixed rope to hope. Hope to return home not only alive, but whole, with fingers, limbs, and mind intact. Spirit unbroken.

PEM DORJEE SHERPA

Pem Dorjee Sherpa was born in Chyangba, a remote village located in the lower Solukhumbu-Everest Region of Nepal. This agricultural village is divided from the rest of the world by nearly impenetrable mountain ranges; hilly, roadless terrain; tangled jungles; and beyond that, space and invisibility. He was raised amidst farmers, goats, and isolation, in an agricultural area just beyond the Everest landscape that has captured the spirit and imagination of the world. His early ancestors migrated from Tibet. Generations of his family were born and raised in Chyangba, his Sherpa name holding the texture of Himalayan stone and high mountain snow deep in its roots.

In Sanskrit, *hima* means "abode of snow" and *alaya* refers to home. The Higher Himalaya region is a landscape defined by its beyond-ness. Its unique topography, with dramatic changes in elevation and diverse climactic conditions, creates a geographic diversity ranging from the tropical alluvial Tarai plains and Siwalik hills in the south to the ice-covered peaks and glaciers and deep gorges of the High Himal. The magnitude of Everest's Mountain systems—its precipitation, altitude, climate, scale, physical threats, and the cumulative risks of climbing—is extreme. The Death Zone, the area above 20,000 feet, is beyond the point where life is sustainable. More than 200 corpses lie frozen in the landscape. Here, extreme cold and heat brews to plus or minus 100 degrees Fahrenheit. Winds gust up to 175 miles per hour, well beyond hurricane force.

Pem is defined by his birthplace, this sacred part of the Himalaya with the wild and mystical Sagarmatha at its center. Like most Sherpas living in the shadows of Sagarmatha, Pem Dorjee Sherpa's decision to summit was not born of hubris. He was not driven to summit by a metaphysical struggle, to test personal limits, or for the adrenaline rush. He did not have the luxury to summit Everest "just because it's there," as Sir Edmund Hillary reportedly declared. Pem attempted the summit out of necessity, to survive.

By the time Pem made his first summit bid in 2004, the Western world's yearning for an Everest conquest had already shaped the economic and environmental culture of the region, inexorably infusing a sense of hopefulness within Sherpa families and villages. There was good money to be made as a porter, though the dangers were extremely high. Even after the 1996 disaster when eight climbers died, more, not fewer westerners sought to climb Everest. Over the years, the commercialization of Everest has brought millions of dollars into Nepal. Yet Nepal remains one of the poorest and least developed countries in the world.

Standing on the shoulders of all other Sherpas who climbed Sagarmatha, feeling the thousands of Sherpa footsteps that passed before him like a river of hope, honoring the sacred mountain and valley soaring above the Imja Khola River and its surrounding peaks—Ama Dablam,

Makalu, Cho Oyu, Lhotse—Pem pursued Everest's summit with the determination and hope of delivering a better life to his family. As a first-born male in a deep-rooted patrilineal, son preference country, providing for his family was Pem's heritage, his duty. He leaned into the Himalaya and prayed, *Om Mani Padme Hum*, and, in exchange for a thin promise, he climbed.

FIRST ASCENT

Pem Sherpa in the Khumbu Icefall, 2004
Altitude:18,000 ft / 5486 m
Photo credit: Kami Sherpa

May 2004

Deep in the Khumbu Icefall, Pem Dorjee Sherpa walked across an aluminum ladder laid across an enormous crevasse, one step at a time, his crampons clawing at the rungs. *Scrape. Clink. Claw.* He waited for his breath to catch up, cautiously lifted one foot, and took another step forward, looking down toward his toes, guiding the crampon teeth squarely onto the rung. The Icefall groaned then shook, reverberating into his bones. *Pop. Whoomp. Boom.* The noise was thundering. His ears rang with the sharp echo. He took another breath. Heart hammering, he stared down through the rungs into the cavernous gap of gray air between two endless ice walls, the only thing between him and death a rickety ladder, two thin ropes, and his wits. His fate hung in the balance of the fickle mood of the Icefall.

The ladder Pem stood on—four sagging aluminum ladders lashed together with rope—had been set across two towering ice seracs and anchored at each end with screws. The ladders had been set at the beginning of the climbing season by the Icefall Doctors. *Would they hold? When were they last checked?* he wondered.

In early spring, the Icefall Doctors, a small group of experienced Sherpa climbers, scout the Icefall to determine the least risky climbing route for the season. They fasten ladders across the crevasses and up and down the ice columns, and fix ropes for climbers on the higher sections of Everest. They test to see if the screws and bolts stay in the ice and the knots tying ladders together hold. It is their job to be judicious. In a place where one twelve-foot ladder appears ideal for a crossing, the ice might be too deteriorated, the path too exposed, forcing them to find a less dangerous route, even if it means lashing four, five, or six ladders together to cross a single crevasse. One shortcut, one small mistake, might mean death.

Pem knew some of the Icefall Doctors and trusted their work. But even the most expertly set ladder could pull out with the thawing and re-freezing of the glacier. Getting through the Icefall alive was one of the biggest Everest gambles.

The ladder swayed beneath Pem's weight plus the fifty-pound pack strapped to his back. He started to wobble. Felt dizzy. He tightened his grip on the safety line. Breathing heavily, he refocused, steadily aligning crampons to ladder step by step, attempting to ignore the mortal risk of the deep abyss and raging ice.

Earlier that morning, as the sun rose across Basecamp, Pem dropped his crampons onto the crusty snow, leaned down and stepped in, one at a time, pushing his toe into the bail, lowering his heel. He looped the straps around his boots and cinched them, tucking the extra strap under itself to keep from tripping. Testing the fit, he stomped around, kicking the snow until the spikes of his crampons held, then stepped warily into the labyrinth of ice.

The Khumbu Icefall, formed by the Khumbu Glacier, the highest glacier on earth, is an intimidating and unforgiving place. Draped between the high shoulders of Mount Everest and Nuptse, the Icefall encompasses a two-mile section of the glacier situated between Everest Basecamp and the Western Cwm (17,900–22,300 feet), the flat cirque below Nuptse, Lhotse, and Everest near Camp I. Ice from Lhotse, Nuptse, and the Western Cwm funnels downslope 1,500 feet through narrow passages and over rocky cliffs before stopping abruptly above Basecamp, the start of the Icefall.

This frozen waterfall is as beautiful as it is dangerous. To begin with, it's a mystical, otherworldly landscape—a dazzling sea of ice-white pyramids, spires, and gigantic slabs of compressed snow rising from stone and reaching for the vast blue Himalaya sky. One of the most startling things about the Icefall and its barren, frozen beauty is the freakishly large scale of the ice formations. Under pressure as the glacier moves downslope about three to four feet per day, tons and tons of ice shifts and contorts, sculpting surprising forms in every imaginable size and shape—a head, monster's teeth, a whale, a Greek goddess. On warm days when a bright sun melts the ice and refreezes, the surface ripples and gleams across the glacier, forming a sea of glittery diamonds that scorch the eyes. Enormous cracks and icy edges catch the light, reflecting startlingly beautiful blue hues.

The glacier's constant movement creates a chaotic, fractured landscape of rapidly changing crevasses. As the sun heats up the steep glacier, the Icefall destabilizes, especially in the more dangerous sections known as the Popcorn Field and Ballroom of Death. Everywhere, a jumble of collapsed pinnacles and skyscraper-sized ice blocks scatter sloppily across the landscape like pieces of a jigsaw puzzle—a reminder that, in an instant, this magnificent, crystallized amphitheater will collapse, reshaping the entire geography, demolishing anything and anyone in the vicinity.

Surviving the Icefall is a matter of odds. The more you climb through, the more likely death becomes your fate. Ladders slip, anchors pull out. Without warning, cornices and seracs break off and crash down the mountain, often triggering an avalanche that sends hundreds of tons of compressed snow, ice-dust, and rocky debris bulldozing down the mountain at high velocity—a living hell for mountaineers trapped in its roaring plume. In 2009, an avalanche in the Icefall killed three local Nepali climbers, and in 2014, took the lives of sixteen

Sherpa climbers who were setting ropes and ladders. Everest closed that year. From Nepal, on Everest's south side, the Khumbu Icefall is both the entrance and initiation to Everest's summit. If your dream is to stand at the top, there is no way around but through, and no route is safe.

Pem was halfway across the ladder when he suddenly grabbed the ropes. The wind kicked up and the ladder bounced wildly, as if a demon was trying to shake him off. He faltered, lost his balance. *Steady,* he told himself. Pem took another step and breathed slowly. He looked down and forged another clumsy step forward, wedging his crampons between the aluminum rails. The Khumbu Icefall, Pem knows all too well, is a place where accidents happen—a slip, a fall, an enormous crevasse suddenly opens, an ice shelf breaks off and a flying chunk of ice the size of a truck wipes out a climber. The Icefall is one of those places on Everest where a climber suddenly questions the merit of taking on the summit.

Pem was particularly vulnerable in the Icefall. Unable to afford a helmet, he climbed without one. Although he had basic mountaineering training, he was green when it came to the Everest summit route. He had never been deep in the belly of the Icefall, never climbed over the most dangerous pinnacles or the last enormous ice tower leading to the Western Cwm. And he had never experienced the Death Zone. This would be his first summit attempt, a first climb as a hired expedition porter.

Standing in the middle of the Icefall on a swaying ladder, an endless void beneath him, Pem was scared.

"I thought I was going to die," he said.

He was a long way from Chyangba Village. How did he get himself in this jam in one of the deadliest places on earth, staring down an endless crevasse, risking life and limb from a ten-story-high overhanging block of ice crashing onto his head? His story began long before he set foot on the shoulders of Everest—a story rooted in a Nepali patrilineal culture and a family myth that holds at its center a tale about his grandfather, a footrace, and a kingdom.

FAMILY MYTHOLOGY

F amily myths and childhood memories are often hazy, disorderly fragments shaped in the mind and played back in vignettes—rich scenes full of accuracies and inaccuracies, their slippery truths often evasive and sometimes buried in family history. The story of Pasang Rinji Sherpa, Pem's grandfather, is one of those murky family tales; a tale that, when pieced together from family members and village elders, goes something like this:

It's a spring day full of light and blossoming warmth in Chyangba. Snow has stopped falling. Frost coats the fallow terraces where maize and potato crops wait for spring planting. In the shed, oxen shift and snort and stomp restlessly, sensing the season to yoke up and furrow the fields.

Pasang Rinji Sherpa is running up a hill in Chyangba along a wooded footpath that curves steeply ahead of him, the sun flushing through the pines and washing over village farmhouses, cornfields and haystacks, the long, winding Solu Sikakhola River now so far behind him it's almost invisible. Breathing hard, his tunic stained with warm sweat, he looks up and down, squinting at the emerging ridges ahead and the landscape at his feet—twisting juniper, red soil, rhododendrons, the vague mist of dawn evaporating over the valley sky. Pasang is gauging the distance to the crest of the hill, being careful to not stumble. His legs are young and strong, his shoulders tight, arms pumping as he labors up the mountain, his feet scarcely touching the earth. Though he can sense other village men running behind him, they seem to be standing still and he sees no one, only the dark, moving shadows cast by overhead clouds. Maintaining a rhythm even in tempo, he crisscrosses the terraced land, reaches the top of the ridge, smiles to himself, and declares victory: Pasang Rinji Sherpa, King of Chyangba.

The story begins back in the days of the monarchy when Nepal was divided into kingdoms. According to Pem, every three to six years there was a footrace to the top of the village mountain to see who would become village king. The footrace tradition is thought to have begun after the death of the Nepali king when the ruling sons could no longer manage large kingdoms. Whoever reached the top first carrying puja offerings for the deity was crowned king.

What Pem knows of his grandfather is incomplete—foggy details gleaned from tales told by his parents and village elders. It is known for certain that at one time, Pasang was crowned king of Chyangba after winning the title in that footrace. Pasang was a hot-tempered, powerful man, ambitious and bold, aloof to his family, yet highly social within the village. Like many villagers, he liked his *chang*, the local alcoholic drink made from fermented grains, and often drank to excess. Although he died at age eighty when Pem's father was just five years old, his presence was felt immensely, his energy shooting straight down through the generations, settling in their bones.

After leaving Tibet, Pasang settled in Chyangba, married Doma Sherpa, and had six daughters. Desperate for a son—a male heir to inherit property—Doma organized a second marriage for her husband when Pasang was sixty years old. For a potential son-bearing wife, she selected a young village girl whom she thought would bring luck and sons and not too much trouble. Their union produced four daughters and, finally, two sons. Although the male heirs were not Doma's blood relatives, she still ruled the household, according to village elders. As one village story goes, Doma made the three-day walk from Chyangba to Jiri with Pasang and his young new wife and family in tow, the new wife on display out in front, her body tense under the village gaze and searing afternoon sun.

Years later, Pasang Rinji Sherpa was arrested. His arrest, Pem believes, came during the time when the war of control between the government of Nepal and local villages had escalated, and the government was forcefully stamping out the ancient footrace tradition. Pasang's wife Doma walked seventy-five miles from Chyangba to Kathmandu to request her husband's freedom, explaining to officials that Pasang was only acting, and not really claiming kingship. Pasang was released, but when he returned to Chyangba, he continued governing the village as if he were king, as if his incarceration had never happened.

Decades later, as the village story goes, Pasang Rinji Sherpa was running again, this time his body leaner, more weathered by life and geography. Now seventy-five, pale and bruised in the face and arms from a police officer beating, he was arrested a second time. He walked from Chyangba village toward the Kathmandu jail with the police officers who had stripped him of his title and kingdom. In village fields, the corn and squash had ripened. Sherpa women were bent over the rich, red earth, digging up the last of the potatoes. Corn stalks in the shape of miniature huts were stacked across the fields, drying. Ravens cawed. Ahead, a lone musk deer browsed at the edge of the woods while an angry wind pushed clouds across the ridge. Pasang's eyes focused ahead as he followed the familiar dips and rises of the hills he knew intimately, places where the woods—thick with Himalayan fir, hemlock, silver birch, and rhododendron—gave way to fields, where the land dropped suddenly. Abruptly, Pasang turned from his captors and ran. He ran downhill in long, uneasy strides, then suddenly veered off the trail. Relieved to be free of an unimaginable reckoning—a slow death in jail—his gods with him, Pasang tossed his head up in the air and dove off the path. The officers' shrill cries echoed through the hills as they ran after him. Stopping at the point where their prisoner was last seen, they peered over the edge to see Pasang lying chest down, impaled on a bamboo scrub below. Motionless and bleeding, Pasang Rinji Sherpa was left alone in the woods to die.

But hours later, Pasang, the outlier who imagined a life different than the one he was born into, got up and walked back to Chyangba.

CHYANGBA, NEPAL

Chyangba sits high on a verdant, terraced hill in northeastern Nepal, an agricultural area 11,482 feet above sea level. According to Pem, the word *Chyangba* in the Sherpa language means "land covered by bushes." Like most villages in Nepal, Chyangba is extremely remote, absent of roads and motorized vehicles. The nearest city, Kathmandu, is about 250 miles away. Various ethnic groups settled there— Sherpa, Rai, Magar, Chhetris, Tamang, Sunuwar, Newar, Vishwakarma, Brahamin—mostly subsistence farmers growing crops of potatoes, maize, wheat, and barley. About 200 stone houses are scattered throughout the village, their blue metal roofs glinting in the sun. Houses are surrounded by grass and cornfields where scarecrows made of sticks and colorful sweatshirts stand tall like sentries. In the fall, Sherpa women can be seen filling baskets with corn husks.

The family home where Pem grew up is a compound of three stone and wood houses. His parents, Dawa and Chhoki, live in the original one-level stone house, and Pem's sister lives in another. The third home, a two-story stone house that Pem built after the 2015 earthquake destroyed much of the village, sits empty. His parents are too afraid to live there. Should another earthquake rattle Chyangba's hillsides, they fear the second story will crumble, crushing them in the rubble. The family cows and goat are tucked in the shade of thatched and tarped pole sheds built at the edge of the cornfield close to the house. In the middle of Dawa and Chhoki's cornfields, grass is heaped on broken cornstalks and left to dry. Cucumbers grow from a makeshift hothouse. Colorful prayer flags are strung along the house, along with rows of corn cobs tied together and hung to dry. In the small yard near the house, chickens stand quietly beneath cone-shaped basket cages, docile in the heat. There is no running water or electricity at the house and the cooking is done on an open wood-fired stove. Water is lugged up from a stream in the lowland. Behind the house, a hole in the ground serves as a toilet.

Nothing about Chyangba changes much over the years and decades due to the lack of transportation and infrastructure. The same families live in the same houses. The same footpaths lead to the small village grocery store, school, and the same stream where villagers fill water buckets. It's possible for village boys to finish school, but not girls. In the twenty-first century, girls are still less valued than boys, often preordained to child marriages or sold into the sex trade. Stocking up on groceries requires the same six-day walk. There are still no motorized vehicles in these villages. Commerce, farming and transporting goods from place to place is conducted by foot on the backs of villagers, or by yak or *zokyo*, a hybrid pack animal, a cross between a yak and a cow. If a sudden life-threatening injury or illness necessitates a medical airlift or a car ride to a Kathmandu hospital, villagers violently throw up from motion sickness. In fact, for this reason, according to Pem, most villagers— particularly the older generation—refuse to go anywhere other than on foot.

Across Nepal, these remote villages remain relatively unchanged unless someone or something intervenes—an earthquake, the gift of a generous philanthropist, a wealthy or famous climber who passes through and feels a connection. Or a local villager achieving off-chance fame, affluence, or influence, usually by summiting Mount Everest or immigrating to another country and pursuing an education that leads to a high paying job. These instances, though, are rare.

From the highest point in Chyangba, in the distance, set far back from the red soil and green hills of the village, a tiny, distant view of the bone white peak of Mount Everest extends upward, shortening the vast blue Himalaya sky. Yet scaling the mythic mountain was not fixed in Pem's imagination like it was with the rest of the world, perhaps because Chyangba was isolated and just far enough off Everest's climbing route. Rarely did word spread about the commerce and work opportunities in and around Namche, and even if it did, parents tried to keep their children working in the fields. Most Nepali children in remote villages lived in persistent poverty; their dreams, if they had them, were stolen by hunger, a forced child marriage, the necessity of work over an education. Having a daily meal of rice, or running water, and a lamp to leave on at night or do homework by, was an extravagance. To most villagers, Everest was a sacred mountain and conquering its summit was reserved for foreigners with options, accumulated wealth, and layers of life beyond ministering to daily essentials. And yet, astonishingly, through a series of planned and unplanned events, Pem would end up challenging Everest's summit, not just once, but twice.

GROWING UP IN THE VILLAGE: SCHOOL DAYS

In Chyangba, the village school sits high on a hill facing the mountains. The schoolhouse has stood there for years, in near view of Everest, Numbur, Makalu, Lhotse, Pikey, and Mera Peaks, their white crags breaking the skyline, weathering monsoons and earthquakes in view of packs of rowdy children. To reach school, Pem made an arduous four-hour walk through narrow, windy village paths, sometimes in monsoons and snowy conditions. His feet nearly bare, clad in flip flops or thin-soled shoes, and wearing the only set of well-worn clothes he owned, he walked to school alone or occasionally with a handful of classmates, traversing steep jungle trails where wild animals prowled. It was easy to get hurt in that mountainous terrain. Sudden rain showers made for slick, gumbo soil. Streams and rivers could rise quickly during a monsoon, and, like most villagers, Pem had never learned to swim.

Pem began the long walk to school after finishing his daily chores of collecting firewood, gathering water from the stream, milking the cow, feeding the goats, and tending to his four siblings; tasks he began before daybreak. After a full day of school, he made the four-hour trek back home, completed a few more hours of chores and as much homework as he had the energy and interest for, and fell into bed.

Chyangba's isolation created challenges for families, especially around education, work, and opportunity. Each year, the cost for Pem to attend school rose higher and higher, until eventually, his mother declared that they could no longer afford to send him. By age twelve, Pem joined the ranks of most Nepali children and became a dropout with an eighth-grade education. Only boys were allowed to attend school, and most left between third and sixth grade, trading school for work. As soon as they were strong enough to work in the fields, they were expected to help support their family.

Parents unable to afford school supplies for their children felt ashamed and pulled their kids out of school because it was easier than facing the judgment of villagers, Pem said. Most village parents had never attended school themselves, including Pem's parents, Dawa and Chhoki. As a result, they had difficulty seeing the value of education in landlocked, impoverished Nepal where, from their perspective, life choices remained perennially limited to the immediate needs of sustaining the farm. Even today, many of these same barriers to education continue in Nepal's small villages, especially for young girls.

Pem was not a big fan of school. After morning chores and a long walk to get there, kids were in school from 10 a.m. to 4 p.m.

"School was hard. I hated it," he said. "I walked four hours to school. That's like trekking from Tengboche to Namche!" he exclaimed, now armed with the knowledge of exactly what each leg of the Everest route demands.

The trek between Tengboche and Namche is a five-hour walk with a 3,000-foot elevation gain. The kids had an hour-long break for lunch.

"Lunch was dried corn mixed with soybean," Pem said. It was a skimpy meal he detested that left him hungry.

Conditions at the schoolhouse were harsh and unsanitary, with no running water or toilet to speak of. Pem recalled a day walking to school with a friend when he was about six years old. On the way, the young boy accidentally pooped his pants.

"When we got to school, the teacher sent him back home. There was no place to wash hands or anything, just a hole in the ground to go to the toilet."

After school, the kids made the long trek home and immediately went to work on household chores. There was little time or energy left for homework, and the low light and foul smell of kerosene lamps made reading difficult.

Being small for his age brought trouble Pem's way.

"I always had to be careful at school. You have to be big, or you get bullied and beaten," Pem said. Even the class monitor beat the kids. School discipline was also harsh. "When we were bad or missed answers, we were beaten with a stick on our hands until they turned blue. If I gave a wrong answer, I had to stand up, cross my arms to opposite ears and stand on one foot for punishment."

At the time, he thought this kind of punishment happened to every kid in school anywhere in the world.

Although school and life at home were harsh, occasionally, there were times when Pem could simply be a mischievous young boy. On rainy days, he played hooky from school and waded in the river with other truant friends.

Once, he and several entrepreneurial friends and cousins stole apples from neighborhood trees and sold them to unsuspecting villagers. With the pocketed rupees, they bought candy, a rare treat. Another time, on his way to school, Pem noticed a set of pots and pans on the trail by the river. The cooking pots had been left during a funeral rite as an offering for the afterlife of the deceased. Pem found a stick in the woods and made a carrying pole, then picked up the pots and pans with the pole and carried them to the river.

"Touching the offerings with bare hands would bring bad karma," he said.

He washed the pots with sand from the riverbed and sold them for fifty rupees. With the money, he treated himself to candy and chang.

The funeral, as it turned out, was for his mother's cousin who had committed suicide by jumping off a cliff. A few days after he was found, the young man's body was brought home for prayer, then cremated. Monks were called in by the family. They sat for fifteen days and spoke to the spirit. For two weeks, the family fed the monks and paid them well to ensure that their cousin's spirit went happily into the afterlife. When the monks' prayers ended, a changing ceremony, or final party, was held in the village, with gifts offered to the young man's spirit. Traditionally, each year, on the anniversary of his death, another celebration is held. It's a challenge to appease the spirit of someone so young, Pem explained.

"When a young person dies you are guessing what will keep their spirit happy in the future. Our cousin might not be happy with what he was given—chicken and gold. If a dead person is not happy, the spirit returns to give the family a hard time—maybe even kill them."

As a boy, thoughts of ghosts and evil spirits haunted Pem.

SHRINDI

rowing up in an isolated and densely forested village with parents who filled their children's heads with frightening stories, darkness became an evil spirit that fueled Pem's dreams and scared him even while he was awake.

To ease their fear of the dark, Pem and his siblings, and cousins, too, slept together—four to six of them jammed into one small bed. While walking around Chyangba at night, villagers carried lit branches as a torch. If a torchlight was seen after midnight, Pem's parents believed it was a walking ghost. If a cat wandered into their house and meowed, someone's ghost had entered with it. Once, Pem recalled, a crying cat entered their house. Pem's mother, Chhoki, believing it was a sign that a witch had entered bringing ill fortune, acted quickly to kill the spirit. After a manic flurry of arm waving to shoo the cat back out, she grabbed a fire stick, lit it in the stove, and chased the cat out with the glowing, smoky ember, yelling in Sherpa:

राति बिरालो कराउदै आएमा बोक्सी आएको भनेर खेदने र घरमा अशुभ हुने भनेर खेदने गरनिछ !

Out, witches! Out, ghosts! Leave us alone, spirits! Away with you!

When someone died in a village home, Pem would avoid that residence for months.

"My heart would beat too much as I walked near these houses where someone died," he said.

To avoid lingering ghosts, he bushwhacked through village woods giving wide berth to these homes. Although the bodies were long gone and the spirit, according to traditional beliefs, was whisked to the afterlife, he was spooked.

"I worried that spirits would find me and cut me up," he said.

According to Pem's Buddhist tradition, after cremation, the spirit is cut off from the living world but remains close by while seeking out a new body and life. *Shrindi*, the lurking ghosts of the dead, walk the same forest pathways as humans, and it is believed that offending them might provoke illness or a lasting intrusion into one's life. In his small boy voice, Pem spoke to the listening universe, begging the spirits to leave him alone.

His fear began with stories his parents told him and his siblings to keep them behaving, but it didn't help Pem's wariness of ghosts the day he learned about an ancient Hindu tradition practiced in Nepal and India. Pem was in the forest with a group of young boys from his village when he first heard about *sati*—widow burning—where a wife, in devotion to her husband, would walk or be thrown into her husband's funeral pyre, burning alive while musicians played loud music to conceal her screams. Later, when his parents talked about sati, his heart would start beating fast, his breath would turn quick and shallow, and his face become ashen with fear. That story always haunted Pem, and with good reason. It wasn't just a horror story. The practice wasn't banned in British India until 1829, and in Nepal not until 1920, but it was still going on many decades later. In 1987, in Rajasthan, India, a father-in-law was acquitted of forcing his daughter into her husband's funeral pyre.

That fear of ghosts was so powerful that, even as an adult, Pem still gets spooked. When he stays in a friend's guest room or in a hotel room, he's afraid to sleep alone.

"I have to leave a light on or the TV until I fall asleep," he said.

The fret of tormentor spirits nagged at him when he purchased a house from a previous owner. To be free of haunting spirits, he realized that he would have to build his own home.

THE ROAD TO JIRI
जीरीको सडक
JĪRĪKŌ SAḌAKA

Cowshed in Pem's family's lower farm field, Chyangba Nepal
Photo credit: Corinne Richardson

Pem woke in the cowshed, in darkness, in a heap of grass. Wind hissing through the shed, rattling the thin timber poles, jolted him awake. Above, stars glinted in the sky, the sun

still hours from breaking over the Himalayan sky. He rubbed his
eyes with his small hands, wiping away dust and hay chaff, and
climbed out into the cold. The thatched shed, a rudimentary
exposed pole and straw frame, sat unexpectedly in a small field
in the middle of a dense forest. In one corner, the shed opened to
a steep, wildly overgrown path leading up to Pem's family home
two miles above. Rising quickly, shivering against the cold, he
shoved his small, bare feet into sandals, tossed the cows a mess
of hay, and started anxiously toward home.

During monsoon season, his parents sheltered their
livestock in the lowland and sent Pem scurrying down the
hill at night to guard the family assets. The shed was designed
for goats and cows on one side, with grass for sleeping on
the other. Arriving in darkness, he felt agitated and exposed,
uneasily spread a tapestry over the grass, and settled in for
the long night. Although the footpath was familiar to Pem—
he walked it many times a day, gathering wood and water on
the lowland terrace, lugging it up to the house—in darkness,
the tangled landscape morphed into the spooky terrain of a
nine-year-old's imagination, the dark moody trees creaking
and swaying and taking on the shape of monsters.

Pem began the steep trek back up to the house at a walk,
then broke into a run, arms pumping, heart pounding. Afraid
of shrindi, he prayed with every cell of his body, *Om Mani
Padme Hum*. He used this protection mantra against the
greatest threats.

"It was so powerful," Pem said, "it felt like I was carrying
a gun."

As he ran toward home in the cool, dewy morning, leeches
hiding under wet leaves attacked him, their small, slick bodies

latching on to his skin so imperceptibly that by the time he noticed, they had already ballooned into ugly black deformities that only a good salting would remove.

By the time he reached the house, shaking and out of breath from fear and the uphill exertion, a thick line of smoke was already rising from the chimney. Out back, the family goat, hearing footsteps in the twilight, rose from its knees and circled nervously around its stake, gazing toward the house, listening for the sound of corn rattling in a bucket. Pem opened the door and found his papa working in the kitchen by lamplight. Today they would leave for Jiri, the agricultural hub of the valley where villagers sell their goods at market—spices, chickens, goats, salt, fruit, candy, and rice. Set up as an agricultural center by the Swiss Government Aid in 1938, Jiri is also known as the Gateway to the Everest Region after Sherpa Tenzing Norgay and Sir Edmund Hillary passed through on their way to Everest's summit.

This would be Pem's first trip to Jiri, or any city, for that matter. He had begged his papa to let him go so he could see the urban novelties that his papa, friends, and villagers had boasted about. His dad would come home from Jiri and say to Pem, "You can see a car!" Pem had never seen a car, motorcycle, or television, or even modern plumbing—toilets, showers, running water—but it was the cars that sparked his interest.

Chyangba to Jiri is a three-day walk. The route, mostly rutted trails as narrow as cow paths in places, traverses the sides of steep mountainous terrain, crisscrossing the reddish Nepal dirt, gummy and slick during monsoon season, and dust-choking in the searing summer heat. They would leave by 5 a.m. to cross certain areas before the sun hit and made it too hot.

"It was worse than the hill to Namche. Five hours uphill in hot sun," Pem said.

At the house, at 3 a.m., Pem's father spread the items they would carry to Jiri across the length of the kitchen table—seasoned potatoes to sell, and the water and food they would eat on the journey: plain potatoes, dried corn, a Nepali version of milk tea called *chay*, and wheat flour and salt to make *tsampa* porridge, and chang, the milky, sweet brew made from fermented highland grains used as offerings, and at special family celebrations and religious festivals.

In the weeks before the trip to Jiri, Pem's mama spent weeks bent over the potato field excavating even the smallest, sweetest potatoes, her fingertips cracked from digging, the creases in her palms stained mineral-red from the Chyangba earth.

"We pick all potatoes, then after the rain, the little ones come up," Pem said.

This season, Pem's family had a small surplus of potatoes to sell at market. In the days before Pem and his father left for Jiri, Pem's mother worked in the kitchen finishing the potatoes for market, boiling small batches over the flames of an open wood stove, stirring the pot while her husband fed wood to the fire. When the potatoes cooled, she seasoned and dried them, then placed them in small cloth sacks to be sold at market.

"Mom fries them if we don't have enough money for food," Pem said.

Or she used them to make curry. At the Okhaldhunga market, two hours south of Chyangba, the potatoes were traded for salt, rice, cooking oil, green chiles, tea powder, and millet.

"My father is good salesman," Pem said laughing as he recounted the story of his papa selling potatoes in Okhaldhunga.

One time, Mama didn't have enough time to dry the seasoned potatoes before bagging them up, but Papa sold them anyway, knowing they tasted bad. He was sitting on a tarp selling his goods when a customer approached, took a bite of potato, and quickly spat it out. The customer got angry and yelled at Papa, "That's sour. No good." My father got angry and raised his voice at the man. "The potatoes were meant to be sour. If you want to buy it, buy it, otherwise don't touch my things." The man bought several bags and left in a hurry, turning back once to look at Dawa. Every time Papa told this story, we all laughed, Mama especially. We saw ourselves as smart villagers making something from nothing.

As they prepared to leave for Jiri, Pem's father gazed at the table, studying the items and the *doko*, the grass basket they would carry the goods in, his eyes scanning back and forth between the items and the basket. To an outsider, it may have looked as if he were procrastinating—waiting for daylight perhaps—but mentally he was strategically balancing the load, a load considerably heavier than Pem's nine-year-old frame, which Pem would carry from dawn to dusk for six days straight.

The loads Sherpas carry on a regular basis are astonishing. After the devastating earthquake of 2015 that shook Nepal from Kathmandu to Mount Everest Basecamp, Sherpas carried building materials for homes, teahouses, and businesses straight up and down the mountain on their backs, sometimes dropping 900 feet in elevation only to hike up 1,900 feet on the seven-and-a-half-mile route from Namche to Tengboche. Some carried 300 pounds, muscling precarious loads of structural steel beams, large wooden doors, and trusses up the steep, high-altitude terrain, the only assistance a *namlo* attached to the load and drawn across the forehead like a bandana. The namlo removes the weight from the back, channeling it smoothly down the spine.

People have often wondered about the remarkable abilities of Sherpas to carry heavy loads and climb easily in oxygen-deprived altitudes. Western advertisers have long co-opted the word *Sherpa* and used it in developing marketing and brand names, promoting the durability of products, wrongly equating the word Sherpa to a job description. While it's true that without using any special techniques, and at extremely high altitude, Sherpa men can carry 90 percent or more of their body weight, with some Sherpas able to carry 175 percent (contrast that to a fit American who carries 25 percent of their body weight), the word Sherpa is *not* synonymous with porter. Sherpa, pronounced *"sharwa"* by Sherpas, represents an ethnic group, a group of people who migrated from Eastern Tibet to Nepal—like Pem's grandfather, Pasang Rinji Sherpa.

Sherpas do in fact have a different genetic makeup than people from lower altitudes. Scientific studies suggest that Sherpas, having lived at high altitude for hundreds of generations, have the ability to produce more red blood cells, which allows for greater oxygen flow to muscles. In essence, their bodies are more efficient at converting oxygen to energy than lowlanders.

When the doko was finally packed with food, supplies, and bedrolls, Pem's father helped him lift it and cinched the namlo as Pem held the thin cloth to his forehead. As Pem heaved the pack higher up his small back to redistribute the weight, his papa made final adjustments, then walked to the shed where the goat, now big enough to sell, continued its agitated circling. His Papa untied the goat from the post and quickly, with complete calm, wrestled the goat to the ground, crossed its legs, and thrust it onto his shoulders, shrugging a few times to balance the goat as it wiggled and settled down. Though not a large man, Dawa, young and in his prime, was strong enough to easily carry the smaller goats all the way to Jiri on his shoulders. The larger goats he had to drag behind him for three days. In the morning darkness, father and son set off for Jiri.

Pem followed his father over the steep terrain and through well-worn shortcuts that bypassed long stretches of easier trail. Bent beneath their loads, Pem and his father made way slowly, the dimly lit house disappearing behind them. They walked uphill and down and up again, sometimes climbing and descending 900 feet in elevation, his father's walking stick, the *tokma*, tamping the earth in a rhythmic beat. Pem kicked rocks in the trail as he listened to his father's chatter.

"As we walked, my father complained about how hard life was. He tried to make me a perfect boy and told me that someday, I had to take Mom on a trip."

Chhoki had never been out of Chyangba. After a while, his father abandoned his grievances and talked about the cars in Jiri, describing them animatedly. Pem's excitement grew, but his father's words gnawed at him in a vague, unidentifiable way.

A few hours later, as he shifted the doko on his shoulders, a disconcerting thought popped into his head: *How could I, a village boy with nothing, following in Papa's footsteps, take my mama on a vacation?* A sense of worry and responsibility crowded his thoughts.

In the coming years, Pem would find himself pondering his father's murky words, sometimes in the morning as he gathered drinking water from the tiny pond near the house before the cows and goats muddied the water, or as he carried wood uphill, while his parents worked the fields. He felt change edge in the way rain comes on in the springtime, subtly altering the entire landscape. Years later, his father's words would take shape in a more concrete way when his papa returned from Kathmandu, pressed an English dictionary into his hands, and said, "You learn English," tapping his finger aggressively on the dictionary. Pem realized then that his father's words were meant to remind him that as the oldest son, someday it *would* be his responsibility to take care of the family. As an eleven-year-old boy, he understood little about what this responsibility truly meant, but in that moment, the realization that he was expected to create an easier life for his family catapulted him straight out of childhood.

After a few hours of steady walking, Pem and his father rested. Dawa let the goat down and stretched his sore shoulders. The sun had begun to slide over the mountain, its soft yellow light washing the stepped farmland and homes perched on the hillside. They shared water and dried corn. Already, only halfway into the first day, Pem's doko felt too heavy. If only he could take it off and lie down flat in the cool, green grass in one of the small villages they passed with their verdant fields and quaint farmhouses with rows of laundry and drying corn. Pem rubbed his small, sweaty hands against his pants pockets—the only pair of trousers he owned—brushing dust off the sleeves of the jacket his mama had sewn together from his sibling's worn-out clothes. Pem did not own a pair of socks, not even in winter. He felt his feet begin to swell.

When they set out walking again, Pem limped through the first few steps. To stop thinking about his hurting feet and the rest of the long walk to Jiri, his mind drifted to the things he might see at the Jiri Bazaar: a car, market stalls crammed with rice, candy, and the sweet bananas he'd heard described, yet never tasted.

Close to dark, they entered a small village of six houses. Pem turned the prayer wheel at the *gompa*, the temple, praying that his feet would stop hurting. They spent the night at a village teahouse his papa knew from his previous trips to Jiri. His father tied the goat outside and bought a meal of lentil curry, *dal bhat*, and rice made by the teahouse owner.

"Having rice was a big deal for us," Pem said.

Normally, they couldn't afford the satisfying staple. At bedtime, they found an empty spot on the floor alongside other travelers, rolled out their sleeping mats, and dozed off.

Before sunup, they rose, bought a cup of milk from the teahouse owner, and made tsampa porridge from the flour and salt they had packed. Dawa repacked the dokos, helped Pem lift his pack, then hoisted the goat to his shoulders. They left the teahouse prepared for another eight hours of walking the empty countryside—down to the lower elevations of farmland

and tree-lined rivers and up the long, hilly paths again, each day climbing another several thousand feet in elevation. They started early to avoid walking the steep terrain in punishing heat. His Papa walked faster the second day and Pem had trouble keeping up. By the end of the day, when they arrived at the teahouse where they would stay for the night, Pem's feet were so swollen he could hardly walk. His father boiled salted water and Pem submerged his feet, soaking them while Dawa drank chang with the teahouse owners.

Early the next morning Dawa examined his son's puffy feet and grunted.

"Stay here, I'll go to market," his father said.

Pem was devastated that he would not see a car and taste bananas. Dawa packed up Pem's doko, hoisted it along with the goat onto his back, and headed for Jiri alone. For days, Pem sat around waiting for his Papa to return, bored silly, dreaming about the cars in Jiri and tossing stones into a field. When his feet had healed enough to walk comfortably, he followed the teahouse owner down the hill to run the *ghatta*, a water mill used to grind corn and wheat. In Nepal, it was common for these kinds of secure jobs to be passed down the male line and the owner's son would someday run the mill.

Days later, Pem's father returned to the teahouse, the goat and potatoes sold, his doko filled with thirty pounds of chili spice, noodles, cooking wells, and a small bag of rice. Before first light, they started the walk back to Chyangba. The sun was burning hot, the trail running either straight up or straight down. To Pem, it seemed as though his papa walked even faster through the heat, even with a heavy pack. They arrived at a teahouse at dark. His father set down the doko and started buying drinks. At first, his papa paid for drinks with cash, but when his rupees ran out, he bartered with items from his doko—cooking wells, chili spice, noodles—goods meant to be sold in the village for family income. Back in Chyangba, products from Jiri were a welcome relief from potatoes and a treat for villagers who could afford to buy them.

From a corner of the teahouse, Pem drank milk tea, eyeing the adults as they talked and danced and drank and drank. Worry clawed at him as his papa's chang glass and doko emptied. He imagined his mama's reaction when they arrived, his father's empty basket and empty pockets after selling their only goat. He flinched at the thought of the fighting and beatings that would follow their arrival. It would be impossible to hide from the spectacle. Now, Pem laughs, remembering past arguments.

"My parents fought all the time. They still fight. They hit each other with sticks and brooms or anything they can find," Pem said. "Once, when I was four or five, my parents had a bad fight. The next day, Dad went to work in the fields and Mom went to bed and slept for seven days."

Being a child, Pem was not allowed to speak out about his father's recklessness and was left alone to brood. Early the next morning, he fell silently in step behind his papa and walked toward Chyangba with mounting uneasiness.

In Nepal, violence and abuse is a commonly repeated story. Village men and women, who do the tough work of subsistence farming which often fails to yield enough to feed a large family, seek energy and relief from poverty and boredom through alcohol, which often leads to violent behavior.

"Everybody in the village drinks," Pem says. "We all drink in my family. My father wakes up at 3 a.m. and drinks, works the farm, comes home, and drinks again. My parents fight with each other all the time. With fists! Sometimes my brother throws fists, too. Still, even today!" he says, his dark eyebrows raising with astonishment.

DAWA SHERPA

Dawa is a leaner, older version of his eldest son. His face is narrower, more bronzed from working in the field, his body more angular than Pem's. They bear matching shining black hair, a no-nonsense haircut, and shapely eyes capped by long, arching eyebrows. Analogous worry lines carve across their foreheads, and their identical impish Sherpa smiles spread across their faces like a family insignia.

Dawa is a hard worker. He rises at 3 a.m. and heads to the fields for a few hours before returning home to put corn into the grinder and make flour so his wife can cook. He has a cup of tea and returns to the field. Dawa was more relaxed than most village parents. He let his kids play and encouraged them to study. But like many villagers, he developed a bad habit of drinking.

Dawa was born in Chyangba village and orphaned at four years old. After his parents died, his uncles raised him, but beat him regularly. There was no school in Chyangba then, and for jobs, only low-paid farm work. At age twenty, following the path of his uncles, Dawa traveled to India to work in the road construction industry for five years. His dream was to return to the village and take over the family property. Once he had saved up 150 rupees (about $2), he returned to Chyangba and bought an old wooden house for 18 rupees. While he labored to restore his new home, his uncles worked behind the scenes to arrange his marriage to a local village girl, Chhoki.

Not long after Dawa married Chhoki, the uncles put their matchmaking skills to work again to marry off Dawa's brother, who had just returned to the village after working in India and Bhutan for fifteen years. The uncles arranged a marriage to Chhoki's sister, finalizing wedding details over a few drinks, a custom that continues even today, according to Pem.

In Chyangba in the 1990s, a young man with 132 rupees in the bank, a house with land, and a new bride was not considered wealthy by any means, but these assets amounted to a solid start for a young village man with no schooling. Back then, the sense of being rich or poor wasn't a mindset that Pem's parents considered. Before the Everest tourism boom, most villagers lived with extremely limited resources. They didn't travel or attend school where disparities would have been more obvious. With no basis of comparison, they didn't equate their physical reality to poverty. The norm in the village was that parents worked the land and had a lot of kids to help, and everyone lived a simple, hardscrabble life. Status was based on whether a villager was a leader or an elder, or on the amount of land a family owned and the number of people working for them.

Since they married at age twenty-one and seventeen, Dawa and Chhoki have lived in the same stone house and worked their small farm every day. They had eleven children, five of whom died young of various childhood illnesses. Pem is the eldest son, followed by Phuri, then Ngima. Lakpa Rinji

Sherpa is the oldest daughter. Their three daughters are Lakpa Rinji, Phurba and Kanchhi.

Customarily, most Nepali children, boys and girls, are named after the day of the week on which they were born, and they fall under the protection of the deity of that day. Pemba is Saturday, Phurba is Thursday, and Ngima, Sunday. A child's middle name usually represents a virtue. For example, Dorjee means a shining light. In another form, Dorje means unbreakable, indomitable. Pem was born on a Saturday, but his name does not follow custom. At the naming ceremony three days after Pem was born, Chhoki let the lama choose her son's name and he chose "Pem" instead of the traditional "Pemba." Names are confusing in Nepal because almost everyone is given one of seven names.

Chhoki, Pem's mother, was raised in Chyangba village, too, and had no formal education. She is short and thick in build, with a round face and dark brown eyes. Her skin is leathery and browned from the sun. Her physique mirrors the mountainous life she leads—rugged, fit, stocky. Chhoki will say that her life was hard—an arranged marriage at age seventeen, the endless farm work, giving birth to and raising so many children, cooking for the family on the open wood stove in the small kitchen, managing the scarcity of food, clothing, money, and time.

At times, Chhoki suffered from depression and experienced suicidal thoughts, though Pem would not understand it as depression until well into adulthood. Because of the associated stigma, mental health wasn't talked about in village communities, and no treatment was available. Now Pem knows that, for his mother, life was sometimes raw, merciless, and cruel in ways he will never fully grasp, though he has certainly endured his own bleak circumstances and sense of hopelessness. Chhoki's complaints about a harsh life on the farm milking cows, cooking, drying corn, and giving birth to eleven children while losing five are harsh and painful—a life with little relief.

At a young age, Pem and his siblings learned to detect the deepening sorrow and despair in their mother's big brown eyes, the shift in her voice and demeanor—a weariness like an immovable stone.

"You learn to recognize the signs and do what you can to make things better," Pem said.

Chhoki had a temper, too, and a harsh hand. Once, when Pem was in fifth grade, he took a penny from his mother's pocket to buy candy, a treat his family could never afford. When she discovered the penny was missing, she went looking for her son, her anger swelling with every step. Terrified, Pem ran toward his grandmother's house. But midway there, near a clump of dense bushes that seemed too scary to pass through, he turned back toward home.

"I spent the night in the goat shed," Pem said. As he recalled the incident, he breathed out softly and laughed. "Next morning Mama found me and beat me bad with a stick. It felt like she tried to kill me." Pem's heart thundered as he shielded himself with his scrawny child arms. "Please, Mama, don't beat me," he said, his hands pressed together in Namaste prayer. "She started beating my hands."

His mother whaled on him, hitting, swatting, and punching until, finally, out of breath and energy, she quit. She had torn at her son without remorse, and just like that, the beating was over, the coin safely in her fist. She stood back, panting heavily, and stared down at Pem.

In Chyangba and other villages of Nepal, child beatings are not uncommon, Pem said.

"Kids become the workforce in Nepali families, that's why families have twelve children. To help work."

Many pairs of arms make lighter work for the family, but village men and women who do the tough work of subsistence farming are often unable to provide enough to feed a large family. Many seek relief from their circumstances through alcohol and a cycle of abuse sets in and becomes a damaging norm. In remote Nepali villages, there is little financial, medical, or social support for mental illness, alcohol abuse, poverty and isolation, and the cycle of violence often repeats in the next generation. No one speaks of the abuse and violence.

"Parents act like they're trying to kill their children when they do something bad," Pem said. "We don't talk about it much, but when we do, my parents seem proud. They laugh and say, 'See, you lived—that's why you're here,' as if their mistreatment had made their kids more resilient."

RUNAWAY

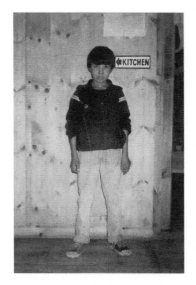

Pem Dorjee Sherpa, Age 12

Pem awoke in stone-cold darkness. Slowly, he swung his scrawny legs over the wooden bench he slept on, and stepped onto the cold, dirt floor. A few feet away, his four siblings were fast asleep on bedsheets of dried corn leaves that smelled like pee, their rhythmic breathing filling the space. Nearby, away from the knot of children, his parents slept on a mattress molded of old clothing, resting their beaten bones—beaten from a lifetime of fieldwork that had calloused their hands, tortured their bodies, and wearied their smiles.

The house smelled of smoke and corn. Quietly, cautiously, Pem crept through the dark, resisting the urge to light a kerosene lamp for fear that he would wake his parents. He sharpened his eyes, took a deep breath, and held it. The path to the door was mostly clear as their traditional Nepali stone home was small and sparsely furnished. Permanent beds were nonexistent. The area where the family of eight slept changed by the season. During corn, barley, and potato seasons, the produce was brought inside to dry, leaving the entire family searching for a place to lay their heads.

Pem worried as he crept through the house. He knew if he got caught, he was done for. The beating would be brutal. If his parents woke, he would pretend he was headed to the toilet—an open pit in the ground behind their home. It was common to be awakened in the middle of the night by one of the adults going out to pee, and he counted on the fact that if his parents noticed his empty bed, they would assume he had gone down to the river or the nearby livestock watering hole to fetch their daily supply of water. Besides, with a head start and no phones, cars, or means of communication except word of mouth, it would be hours before they heard news of their runaway son.

When Pem reached the door, he quickly put on his coat and backpack, slipped out, and ran like the wind. Twelve years old, with just the clothes on his back and a handful of rupees in his pocket—school money he had "borrowed" and stashed away—Pem left his village, his family, and the only home he had ever known. He cut out with no goodbyes. Left no note. No hints of a runaway location. Leaving nothing behind but a twelve-year-old's absence, Pem left for good, and ran north toward Namche Bazaar and the heart of Everest, the light patter of his feet filling the night, the smell of marigold and woodsmoke hanging in the air.

Stars stretched over the Chyangba hillsides and terraced fields below the house where his parents would soon be hunched over their crops—exactly where he would be too, had word of his plan slipped out. Soon, his father would rise, build a fire, and make himself a cup of hot tea or chang, and pack a lunch before heading to the fields. Chhoki would rise a little later, make tea for the younger kids, and shoo them out the door for their long walk to school before milking the cow or heading to the fields to join her husband. Had they caught their son sneaking away, after a blistering beating, they would have kept him at home planting, harvesting, and looking after the family livestock and his younger siblings. Pem was an economic asset to his family, who were always in need of an extra hand.

As he ran toward the Solu Khola River below his house, his only companions were the dozing birds and animals he may have startled awake—jackals, cuckoos, chickens. The further he got from the house, the more he let himself feel the excitement of what lay ahead, even though he didn't know much about the people living closer to Everest or what the villages were like.

Fifteen minutes later, out of breath, his heart pounding, he spotted his friend Dawa waiting at the river, exactly as they planned. He felt a wave of relief. Dawa, a classmate, and about the same age as Pem, had already been to Namche and worked a couple of seasons. He knew the route and had made solid work connections, and his knowledge and survival sense put Pem at ease. After exchanging a happy greeting, the two quickly set out for Namche Bazaar before the break of day.

NAMCHE

L ying in the shadow of Everest, Namche Bazaar is a small market village in Solokumbu, the main trading center and tourism hub for the entire Khumbu Region of Nepal. Known as the gateway to the high Himalayas, it is the last outpost for supplies and the first acclimatization point for climbers before challenging Everest's summit. From Chyangba, Namche is a three-day walk through the villages of Phaplu, Kharikhula, and Lukla, but it would take Pem and Dawa longer to get there. Neither boy had packed food, so they stopped in a small village of fifteen houses where they worked long enough to feed themselves.

Thirty years ago, as a boy, Pem experienced Namche as a small but nice village, not fancy by any means, but having a lot more going on than Chyangba even though living conditions were basic and most local villagers still worked the fields as subsistence farmers or worked as seasonal guides. The village seemed bigger, more active, more affluent than Chyangba, the home decor more attractive and plentiful. Pem observed right away that each household owned far more pots, pans, and serving plates than his family, signifying a level of affluence that was foreign to him. *Wow, nice place*, he thought when he entered the large rooms with their fancy dishes in the teahouses he worked in. Unlike Chyangba, Namche was lit up by electricity that ran at certain hours of the day. In 1992, you could find a hot shower in Namche, big dining rooms, one black and white TV that villagers crowded around, and a tiny screen-projector movie hall to enjoy on Fridays and Saturdays if you had 5 rupees, about one cent, to spare. According to Pem, in the early 90s, most tourists were part of well-organized hiking and camping trips staying in the few small teahouses in the Everest region along with a handful of small expedition groups attempting Everest's summit.

Historically, in the time before Tenzing Norgay and Sir Edmund Hillary's 1953 summit, Namche was a trading post where Sherpas exchanged yak cheese and butter for other agricultural goods. The years between 1953 and 1988 saw the boldest pioneering climbs seeking new routes to Everest from the north and south side of the peak, with a total of about 200 people summiting. By the 1990s, more permits were being issued by the Nepali government and successful expedition operators started bringing ten or more Everest climbing expeditions per season, increasing the number of climbers reaching the summit. In 2007, 630 climbers successfully summited, and more than 800 did so in 2018.

Today, Namche is one of the most modernized, affluent districts in Nepal, with well-stocked stores, abundant Wi-Fi, and bakeries that sell lattes, donuts, and collectible Starbucks coffee mugs. There are even brewpubs in Namche, a North Face store, and a five-star hotel. The village draws hordes of foreign climbers and trekkers, as well as young Nepali kids like Pem from remote villages who flee poverty or abusive homes or are pursuing bigger dreams in search of a way out.

Approaching Namche, the first thing you notice are its colorful houses—red clay, steely blue, forest green—perched above the town on the hillside in tiered rows of blue and green painted windows and colorful vertically seamed rooftops. The horseshoe-shaped village is built into the hillside, high up, at 11,286 feet. Upon entering the village, one passes a traditional, white-domed stupa, the giant, all-seeing eyes of the Buddha staring down. Above the wisdom eyes, painted in yellow-gold, are the thirteen steps of enlightenment. In the Buddhist tradition, the stupa is the focal point of worship. Each village has its own stupa, which varies in size, shape, and decoration from place to place. Typically shaped in a hemispherical mound, the stupa represents the burial mound of the Buddha. Carved symbols of the Buddha and his teachings often appear in scenes throughout the stupa. Prayer flags strung along the outside flutter in the breeze, carrying prayers to the heavens, and mani stones and sacred prayer wheels line the stupa's entrance. Wound inside each cylindrical prayer wheel are sheets of prayers with thousands of printed mantras blessed by a Buddhist lama, including the favored mantra found on most prayer wheels in Nepal, *Om Mani Padme Hum*—a message of spreading loving kindness and compassion.

When Pem and Dawa finally arrived in Namche, Pem was tired and dusty from the long walk. Entering the village, he stopped at the stupa and spun the mani wheels clockwise to activate the blessings and create good karma.

"If you take a wrong turn," Pem said, "you don't feel comfortable. You have it in your mind you will receive bad karma or something bad would happen."

Reflecting on some of the rituals that he performed when back home in Nepal, he said, "The sad part is that I did it, but didn't know why."

While walking, whenever Pem encountered water or crossed a bridge, he would drop a *khada*, a traditional ceremonial scarf, given to him by a family member for protection, into the stream. "The gods stay at those places offering a safe journey."

With Dawa's connections, Pem found work right away with Lhakpa Tenzing Sherpa and his wife, Nima Doma Sherpa, at their two teahouses. His job was to help with household chores—gathering water and firewood, carrying things to neighboring villages, running errands for the owners.

Lhakpa Tenzing Sherpa had extensive experience in the Everest tourism industry though he had never attempted the summit himself. He had been a trekking guide for fifteen years before he and his wife opened teahouses in Namche and Tengboche to service the growing number of trekkers and climbers. Lhakpa's father had been a porter in the 1953 expedition with Tenzing Norgay and Sir Edmund Hillary, and was the only remaining living team member from that expedition, but because so many of his relatives had met their deaths in the climbing industry, his mother had forbidden Lhakpa to climb. The money was good, and tempting for most villagers who had so little, but once Lhakpa married, his wife, Nima, also admonished him, "*No climbing!*" To these women, the risk was not worth the money.

"When Pem first arrived in Namche, he was so small he was unable to carry much of a load," Lhakpa said.

Until he grew, there was no opportunity for Pem to earn the kind of money porters made carrying gear and guiding tourists and climbers up Everest. For now, he could only watch the porters come and go longingly while he labored with the more mundane chores of collecting firewood from the jungle and buckets of water from the stream for washing dishes and laundry and offering the daily prayers. Pem recalled his feelings as a twelve-year-old runaway:

> I had more excitement than fear. I was so excited to make money and eat better food. I was quietly sneaking out of the house. At first, I feel normal, then my whole body reaction changed. I feared if they caught me, my parents might beat me badly and I'd never get the chance to go to Namche again. But then I sneaked out. As soon as I ran, I think they're not gonna catch me. I think if I get up there one time and come home with money, then going back and working is not going to be a problem. They'll send me back to work more officially, sending me off with a khada and food for the walk because the oldest son making money is good for the family.

In the first few years working in Namche, Pem noticed that it was becoming a trend for young boys to leave home and come to the village to work, even encouraged by parents. By the mid to late 1990s, it had caught on that children could make more money in the tourism business than they might bring in at the family farm.

"My dad really wanted me to go to school to educate myself. He tried his best," Pem recalled.

His mother, though, saw things differently. The rising cost of school became a financial burden and when Pem was old enough, she expected him to work and help support the family.

I didn't feel bad leaving home. Working was not a big deal. In Namche, you wake up and have breakfast and lunch. The only difficult time I had was getting wood and carrying loads for six to seven hours. But you're not by yourself. Mostly with similar age boys. It was much more fun than working by yourself at home. You can eat, drink anywhere you go, and you're not told no. It's like a teenage life. When we were working, we slept all the way down at bottom floor. Every night we left a window open and snuck out to play cards and went to market and snuck back into window.

It wasn't that Pem discovered the lost boyhood he was deprived of in Chyangba or felt like he had a lot more freedoms in Namche, even though he did in many ways. Like at home, it was all work, work that was just as physically demanding and menial.

"All of us boys were watched to see if we completed our chores on time," he said.

In his first year in Namche, a normal day began with an early wake-up followed by a day filled with chores.

I wake up. Make tea. Get water. It took fifteen trips to get drinking water. Lhakpa had a huge water pot to fill—maybe 200 gallons of water and I carry about 20 gallons each time. I do all the laundry. Make lunch. Again, go get water. Work in the field. It's like scheduled work but I was kind of happy to do it. So many things are happening, we don't feel bored or miss home.

In Chyangba, Pem's biggest responsibility was taking care of his four siblings, a chore he loathed.

"There's an older gentleman in Chyangba village. He kept telling me how nice I was to take care of kids," Pem said. "We go try to hunt birds, snakes—village kind of things—but we had no toys. I still complain because I had to carry them and sometimes they peed on my back! I kept carrying them and let the pee dry there," he reminisced, laughing.

In Namche, like in Chyangba, there were no toys and few opportunities to play, but what was different, Pem explained, was the camaraderie and the variety of work routines that made it more exciting and interesting for a young village boy. Every morning, in the wee hours, one of the village kids would blast out an ear-piercing finger-whistle and fifty or sixty boys would simultaneously dash out of their houses and converge at the edge of the forest to gather wood. By that time, Pem would already have eaten breakfast, packed a lunch, and gathered water for the teahouse and Lhakpa's daily *puja* offering to the gods. At the sound of the whistle, Pem raced to the meeting point and headed into the steep, forested jungle with the other boys to collect wood.

One of his first big jobs for Lhakpa was to cook for the July festival, *Dumji*, honoring the anniversary of Guru Rinpoche's birth on the lotus flower. Lama Sangwa Dorji, founder of the first monastery of Khumbu, began the festival in Pangboche Monastary 365 years ago. The festival brings the communities of Tengboche, Namche Bazaar, Khumjung, and Pangboche together, and each year, eight local families provide food and drink for the entire village for the celebration. During the festival, a roaring fire is built and young monks play horns while Tengboche monks perform masked dancing with swords. The festival is mainly to purge evil spirits from the villages and worship the patron deity of the Khumbu region. The chosen host serves food and drinks to all the villagers, and that year, Pem was sent to work for the host. It was days and days of endless, tiring, hard work, he said.

On Fridays, Pem's job was to buy items at the Namche market and carry them to Tengboche, a hilly, 6.2-mile trek with an elevation gain of 4,000 feet. On one Friday, Pem was responsible for carrying a heavy load of firewood all the way to Tengboche. Lhakpa's mother-in-law was loading her zokyo pack animal with wood and other items and when she realized that Pem was heading for Tengboche and ordered him to take her zokyo and supplies with him. Pem watched closely as she loaded both sides of the zokyo.

"I saw how slow moving the zokyo was and the nice behavior it had," Pem said.

Once out of sight of Namche, on a flat section of the trail, Pem stripped the load of wood from his back and strapped it on the zokyo and followed it up the trail toward Tengboche, happy and carefree. On this particular trek, he always stopped for lunch at the river, but while Pem was enjoying lunch, the zokyo drifted away and was lost. When he arrived in Tengboche, a villager told Pem where he could find the zokyo—about an hour away from the river, in a pasture where herders put the zokyos out to graze. But it was too late. Unbeknownst to Pem, a passing

Sherpa took notice of the light and carefree boy herding the overloaded zokyo and ratted Pem out. Lhakpa's mother-in-law found him and furiously scolded him. She was so mad, she sent Pem straight back to Namche as punishment for losing both her zokyo and her goods. Feeling sorry for him, the mother-in-law's daughter snuck him a piece of coconut cookie. Happy for the sweet treat, Pem accepted the cookie and left for Namche. He took his time making his punishment lap back to Namche, figuring that if he showed up late, he wouldn't have to work. Sure enough, he reached Namche at 6:30 p.m., and went directly to the movie hall and watched a show.

On the business side of their work arrangement, the boys had no formal contract with their employer. They were paid either at the end of the season, the end of the year, or when they returned home for good.

"We were told that we would get paid later because we'd only spend it," Pem said.

The boys could request a few rupees for pocket change or for a portion of their salary to send home, but beyond that, the boys received no income until the employer decided to pay according to a loosely defined "season." There were some unscrupulous teahouse owners who never paid their employees, but word spread about them. Most boys worked seasonally and returned to their villages in the off-season, and workers who had been mistreated often changed jobs each season. According to Pem, many workers in the Namche tourist industry changed jobs frequently or went back to their villages to work the farms, although occasionally there was an outlier.

"It's hard to believe, but some workers stayed twenty years and even died working at a teahouse!"

Pem worked at Lhakpa's teahouse for two years, earning 800 rupees, about $10 per month. About six months into his job, he began requesting small amounts of money to send home, occasionally requesting an advance if his family experienced dire need. Often, it took a few days to arrange for the money to be transferred to Pem.

There was no mail service to Chyangba, so packages were sent home with a trusted fellow villager who happened to be walking back to Chyangba. For the better part of two years, Pem was out of communication with his family.

"I wrote letters that got sent home with money," he said. "Sometimes I sent a picture, but I never got a reply because my parents don't write."

Pem kept track of his earnings on paper, and at the end of his two-year service, checked it against Lhakpa's records. Fortunately, he worked for a good employer and received all that was due.

THE DEATH ZONE

May 2004

Back in the Khumbu Icefall, Pem reached the end of the four lashed-together ladders. He breathed a sigh of relief, but there was no time to relax, speed is of the essence in the Icefall. As quickly as possible, he advanced through the next series of ladders, seracs, ropes, and ice walls, about eight in all. A strong climber can get through the Khumbu Icefall in about two to three hours, while inexperienced climbers take eight to twelve hours, and are at greater peril as the ice heats up and the glacier moves.

Finally, four hours after stepping into the Icefall, Pem reached the last ladder, a two-story vertical climb straight up a wall of ice. Climbing over the top, exhausted, he removed his crampons, planted his feet on the Western Cwm—the long, flat valley below Lhotse—clipped into a rope and climbed toward Camp I. At 21,000 feet, Camp I made Everest Basecamp feel like a cakewalk. Here, breathing is a substantial chore, moving even more cumbersome, thinking diminished—conditions that would only worsen when he entered the Death Zone, the area above 26,000 feet where human life is unsustainable. Caught there more than a few days, and you're dead.

The Death Zone is a formidable place—the cutoff for human consciousness without supplemental oxygen; a place where one could essentially sleep to death. At this altitude, the human body shuts down. Digestion ceases, lungs swell. The heart beats 140 beats per minute, in contrast to a normal 60 to 100 beats. It feels like your heart is going to explode out of your chest. Adrenals fail. Cognition and memory fail. This is a place where you feel wholly unlike yourself. Death can happen on the way up or on the way down, which is even more likely, or on a rest day, and even while sitting still, which, at 26,000 feet, is strenuous exercise. It can happen to anyone, anytime, anywhere despite experience, training, and fitness. Some fatality rates estimate that one in twenty-five climbers die in Everest's Death Zone.

In the Death Zone, the mind forgets the simplest of things, like eating and hydrating, and the critical, matter-of-life-and-death kinds of things, too, like safety checks and conducting your daily summit checklist. *Are my boots secure? Crampons on? No skin exposed? Can I feel my feet? My hands? Did I pack energy food and water? Is my headlamp positioned correctly for the summit? Is my oxygen tank turned on and the line feeding properly and not frozen? Where did I stash those spare oxygen tanks for the descent?*

The use of supplemental oxygen, while necessary for consciousness, offers little other protection against the demands of the Death Zone. Extra oxygen won't prevent acute mountain sickness, the headache, nausea, dizziness, and insomnia that sets in with decreasing levels of oxygen, or HAPE, high-altitude pulmonary edema that occurs when altitude sickness causes the lungs to fill with fluids. Nor will it prevent HACE, high-altitude cerebral edema, where the brain, swelling from excess fluid, is literally being squeezed out of the confinement of the cranial cavity. Diminished oxygen supplies and a flooded brain can cause wild hallucinations that coerce a perfectly rational, healthy person into crazy acts, like madly peeling off your clothes in sub-zero temperatures in the false belief that it's a singeing 90 degrees. You don't see it coming. It sneaks in like a snake in the grass. A day ago, you thought you were simply breathing hard, but today, with a dangerously low level of oxygen and flooded lungs, you are coughing up a pink, frothy mucus, blowing bubbles through your nose, and feel as if you can't breathe in any air at all. More than five miles above sea level, you are drowning and at the same time suffering all those indignities as the body slowly dies, the ribs broken from a violent cough or sneeze because breathing Everest's cold air dries out and cracks the lung lining. Muddled thinking leads to poor decisions or dangerous hesitations, decreased coordination, and the inability to walk. Relentless diarrhea, vomiting, headaches. A bony, nutrient-starved body. Blood vessels in the eyes hemorrhage, causing pain and blindness. Corneas are burned by the sun's glare on the snow, leading to very painful snow blindness. Frostbite. Hypothermia.

In an advanced hypothermic state, the body's senses are tricked into feeling hot, sending it into terminal burrowing behavior, a form of primitive hibernation. Hypothermic climbers have been known to strip off their clothes in the irrational belief that they are hot. Some climbers have been found in a crevice or wedged under a rock with clothes missing or stripped down to undergarments, or even bare skin. Climbers experiencing acute hypoxia and hallucinations have jumped off cliffs, talked to invisible companions, even fought off Sherpas trying to help them safely down Everest, seeing monsters instead of humans. Hypoxic climbers have simply wandered off, never to be seen again.

Mostly, you hear about these misfortunes happening to westerners, but altitude sickness can affect Sherpas, too.

FIRST SUMMIT

Nawang Sherpa, the first person to scale Everest with a prosthetic leg

At 17,500 feet, Pem held his client's left leg in his cold hands, pivoted the un-flexing limb right, then left, and stared at the shiny, rawboned muscle of the prosthesis. Pondering its functionality and mechanics, he packed the prosthesis in his rucksack—two and a half pounds of titanium and carbon fiber fitted with a specially designed crampon. He wondered how this client would do attempting Everest's perilous summit with an artificial leg, how he'd fare on a wind lip or snow cornice, a hidden crevasse, or crossing the Khumbu Icefall's towering pinnacles and bottomless crevasses on wobbly aluminum ladders tenuously pinned to a shifting glacier. Could he recover from an inevitable slip and fall? How would he accomplish these grueling, exacting efforts made in extreme high-altitude conditions without reflexes and sensation, without the ability to know—*without feeling*—exactly where his thigh, calf, shin was in space, how fast his leg was moving, and with what degree of exertion and force? Calibrating every move is one of the many no-room-for-error demands of climbing Mount Everest's unforgiving terrain. When the oxygen-starved brain becomes disoriented, one hopes all parts of the body will perform on autopilot and rely on muscle memory.

Not long before Pem stepped into the Khumbu Icefall, he received his porter assignment. He had been hired to join a summit expedition organized by Nepal Peak Promotion, an expedition company owned by Wongchu Sherpa, an accomplished mountaineer from Pem's home village of Chyangba. Remarkably, Wongchu had set a record for staying above 22,965 feet for eighteen consecutive days. Over the years, he had built a successful commercial expedition company that also specialized in filming, having worked on high-profile films including the *National Geographic* documentary *Surviving Everest* and David Breashears' *Everest.*

Peak Promotion's client, American climber Tom McMillan, and his thirty-three-year-old teammate, Nawang Sherpa—an Everest trekking guide until he lost his leg when his motorcycle crashed into a bus in Kathmandu—had hired Wongchu's company to help them triumph over Everest. If the team made it to the top of the world, Nawang would be the first person to scale Everest with a prosthetic leg and Pem would have his first Everest summit. As an expedition porter, Pem's job was to securely deliver the client's prosthetic leg from Basecamp through the Death Zone to Camp IV (26,300 feet)—the last camp before the summit and first safety-rest point upon descent. In addition, Pem was the designated expedition cameraman and videographer from Everest Basecamp to the summit, assigned to capture ragged endurance shots and icy, death-defying scenes in the Khumbu Icefall and Death Zone, as well as conquest shots from the summit if the team succeeded.

After years of backbreaking work running between Namche and Everest Basecamp as a low-paid porter, Pem was ready for change, and the job paid well. He was twenty-two, unfamiliar with the upper Everest summit route, but eager for the experience.

"It felt a bit strange," Pem said of being responsible for a client's prosthetic leg, which was as critical a factor in the climb as oxygen.

Peak Promotion's expedition leaders had thoughtfully anticipated and prepared for a variety of problems during the expedition and had arranged for a spare prosthesis to be carried up the mountain in addition to the prosthetic leg the client wore, and the replacement in his backpack. Pem signed on knowing that his performance could determine the success or failure of this expedition and that life or death could rest in his hands.

Adding to the stress of his first summit as a porter, a tremendous amount of energy and hype surrounded Everest at the time, with the high-profile expedition led by two of the most famed and respected elite mountaineers, David Breashears and Ed Viesturs, underway. The veteran climbers were taking a team to the summit to begin filming *Everest*, a documentary about the May 1996 storm that killed eight climbers, and the subject of Jon Krakauer's book, *Into Thin Air*. Breashears had been filming on the summit in 1996 and had descended with his team the day before the catastrophic storm hit and volunteered with rescue efforts.

When talking about his first summit, Pem had difficulty recalling the details and his emotions about making it to the top. Chuckling, he said, "I don't remember a lot about it. It was all so new and scary. The Khumbu Icefall, the Death Zone. I had a hard time. Had never used crampons before, and no one told me how to go through the Icefall. No one instructs you—you learn on the job. There were no mentors, only a minor verbal briefing from the expedition team. And no helmets!" he exclaimed.

What he does remember in hazy detail, were the firsts: the unique task and responsibility of delivering someone's *leg* through the Death Zone to the summit; his first time through the terrifying Khumbu Icefall; learning how to use crampons just a few days before the expedition; and the long, snaking line of climbers below the summit. Major bottlenecks from the South Col to the Balcony just below the summit were a problem even back in 2004, Pem noted. That was long before climbers carried GoPro cameras and captured the now famous photo, published in a May 2019 *New York Times* article, showing an absurd line of more than 300 climbers jammed along the spine of Everest in the Death Zone.

Pem recollects the way he and other Sherpas drank to forgetfulness at the end of each climbing day to deflect their fears, fears that came fast and furious, especially going into the Khumbu Icefall and Death Zone. He remembers the tangled spaghetti of fixed ropes on the trail above Camp IV, south of the summit.

"To be safe, you have to find the good rope. But you just grab everything—four, five ropes—you grab them all," he said. "I try to grab one that looks a little nicer!" he said with a laugh.

From Camp IV's Death Zone, where Sherpas and climbers use supplemental oxygen, it's too hard to bring old ropes down, Pem adds. Usually, on the upper mountain, a team of Sherpas will set and check ropes a few days before the first expedition plans a summit bid, but if they think a rope is safe, they leave it in place jumbled with all the others. On the way to and from the summit, hundreds of climbers tug and hang from the fixed ropes, increasing the chance of a fixed rope pulling out. Only in the Khumbu Icefall are ropes checked daily, Pem said, recalling the six-section vertical ladders they climbed in the Icefall that year. That same year, the upper section of the Icefall broke off in an avalanche. Fortunately, no one was killed.

Pem remembers deliberately setting out for the summit ahead of Peak Promotion guides and the client, the camera equipment and the client's prosthetic leg stowed in his backpack. His work instructions for that day were to follow behind the group as additional support, but instead, he went for the summit on his own.

"I knew clients often never made it to the summit, and I badly wanted to make it," he said. But as it turned out, he found the summit climb so tough, Pem swore that summiting would only be a once or twice occurrence, not his career calling.

The dreaded Death Zone is permanently fixed in Pem's memory: how his breath shortened, leaving him continuously gasping for air and feeling a "tight squeeze" in his chest. It took thirty minutes to put on climbing boots and every step was an exhausting event. He puffed and panted while he slept, if he slept, and never felt warm, despite layers of down. The supplemental oxygen's effect was not what he expected. It provided no boost of energy and performance and offered only a slight offset to the extreme exertion.

"The oxygen didn't help my energy," he said. "It only made it a tiny bit easier to breathe." The reality is, that every minute in the Death Zone, the body continues to lose mass, strength, and endurance with, or without, bottled oxygen.

Pem remembers a general feeling of excitement stepping onto the summit, and noticed how expansive the views were across Tibet and Nepal, how small some of the peaks looked. But few other concrete details and emotions of that day standing at the top of the world remain. He distinctly remembers not getting paid for that day's work because of dereliction of duty, even though Nawang made it to the top and Pem filmed the team celebrating at the summit. After the expedition returned to Basecamp, Pem, at age twenty-two, was celebrated as the youngest Peak Promotion staff member to summit Everest.

And he clearly remembers calling Moni Mulepati, the girl who had captured his heart just a few months earlier.

"Moni, you can do this," he said panting into the satellite phone, the wind whipping around him on the summit.

Pem first laid eyes on Moni in the winter of 2003 while he waited to interview for a spot in the Advanced Mountaineer training class held at Yala Peak.

"I was the last one to interview, and that's when I first saw her. I noticed her right away—the skirt, boots, and nice legs," Pem said, smiling, eyebrows raised. "She was like a movie star."

In a classic *Jerry Maguire* moment, Moni Mulepati had him even before "hello." Despite being smitten, Pem was skeptical of a woman guide, especially on Mount Everest.

"I looked at Moni and the two other women applying and thought, these women aren't going to make it! If I didn't get into the course, I would be mad!"

PART II

MONI MULEPATI
NEWARI REBEL

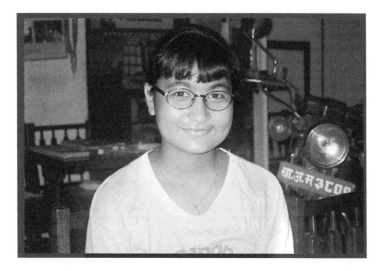

Photo Credit: Moni Mulepati

Moni's Words, November 2020

Before marriage, we are controlled by the father, then after marriage, by our husband, and when we get old, controlled by the son. I wanted to break rules and barriers, to do something—make something of myself beyond marriage, beyond raising babies. In our culture most men and families would say they don't want that girl wearing a skirt—she's promiscuous, a rule breaker. I wanted more freedom than what I saw my married cousins had—what my mother had. I wanted to be loved.

When I was a child, my family owned a guest house and restaurant, and I would see foreigners coming with big backpacks to go trekking and hiking. I knew nothing about it, but I wanted to go. But being a woman in Nepal, you can't go out from home camping, or socialize with other people. I saw a lot of different people from Germany, Japan, France, USA—all around the world. When they come down for tea or dinner, I talked with them. They found me friendly like my daughter, Mezel. I helped them with their things, and they became my friends. When they went back home, they sent letters and gifts. One of my Japanese friends sent me a cartoon watch, which you don't find in Nepal. I feel very special.

I always dreamed when I saw an airplane and wondered when I could travel. My first flight I ever took was when I was sixteen when I went to Bangkok to study. First plane ride ever! It gave me more vision.

TRAINING
ANNAPURNA BASECAMP

December 2003 – Spring 2004

What began it all was, in all probability, an inventive childhood combined with a spirited disdain for cooking and arranged marriages. Mountaineering had not pulsed through the Mulepati family veins like it had in the family of, say, a Jamling Tenzing Norgay. Yet here she was, back home in Nepal after quitting university studies in Thailand, signed up for mountaineering classes, unwittingly setting herself on a course to conquer a challenge at the outer limits of danger: Everest. Patriarchy.

Raised in a traditional middle-class Newari Hindu family near the capital of Kathmandu, Moni spent her childhood helping her father, Mohan, in the family's guest house located on Freak Street in Jhochhen Tole, an artsy tourist hub in the historical part of Kathmandu Valley near Durbar Square Basantapur. A hippie paradise in the 1960s and 1970s with its legal hashish shops, Jhochhen is now quieter. Shopping and an active nightlife attract tourists, trekkers, and elite mountaineers.

In the colorful traditional interiors of the Himalaya's Guest House, Moni took respite in her favorite spaces—the check-in area with its colorful aquarium, seventeen guest bedrooms, a reading room, and her favorite—the restaurant café with its seventh-floor terrace where her father had placed ornate plantings he had made in drums, juice boxes, and cans. Just outside the door, Moni played and bargained with shopkeepers in the enchanting open courts of Durbar Square, the former Kathmandu Kingdom of the Malla and Shah Dynasty.

Durbar Square means the "palace of the prince" and is an open court lined with sixteenth century palaces and pagoda temples carved by esteemed Newar artists and craftsmen. Moni floated through the narrow and congested red brick streets bustling with small shops and open stalls, souvenir vendors, and money exchanges, weaving in and out of the places she knew well, gazing with wonder at the water fountains and stone-carved statues of the gods and lions and watching the throngs of tourists with their strange outfits and languages with curiosity.

A strong-willed and curious child, Moni was a nuisance and source of consternation to her parents, especially her mother, Shanti, always bending, pushing, twisting, rejecting, or outwardly breaking the rules, though always in a no-nonsense, rational and dignified way. As a young girl, she was enthralled with the swarms of foreigners who visited their guest house and spent most of her time working beside her father while her siblings, for the most part, stayed home.

Her father had a soft spot for Moni.

"Moni was a quiet child, unlike her sister Soni, who was into everything and was hungry all the time," he said smiling.

"Moni never cried, even when hungry. She was also tough. She was a hard worker and had a business brain from a young age. She collected money from the counter at our teahouse. She had a good mind and good ideas."

The second oldest of four, Moni would slip into the eldest role when her older brother died unexpectedly as a young boy. Traditionally, only boys inherit, but with her brother's premature death, in a subtle, undeclared way, Moni assumed the role of eldest son—to support and run the family and make the family proud.

The Himalaya's Guest House was small, but popular and steadily booked. Sometimes after school, when the guesthouse was busy and her mother was working in the restaurant, Moni and her sister, Soni, would join the chairs together and sleep amidst the clatter of dishes and steady hum of foreigners, the strange energy and excitement fueling Moni's dreams.

Moni's grandpa made yoghurt in Bhaktapur, which laborers carried to Kathmandu on bamboo sticks and ropes, delivering batches to the restaurant for her father to sell.

Her father, Mohan Mulepati, was a traditional Newari for the most part. He comes from a long line of business owners from Bhaktapur. His father, Monish, was a self-made, successful businessman. The Newar caste, whose occupations include farmers, prominent retail traders, officials, and artisans, are indigenous to the fertile Kathmandu Valley, having settled in the medieval towns of Kathmandu, Patan, and Bhaktapur, part of the Newar Kingdom until 1768.

Moni describes her father as a hard worker, a provider for his family, and a businessman. Every day, he rose at 4 a.m. to open the restaurant and ran both the family business and their home. Mohan highly valued education for his children and was strict, especially about school.

"If you saw red mark in grade book you were dead," Moni said, wagging a finger. "Dad never missed a conference. If he heard any negative information, you were gone, and we got spanked very hard. If my sister got in trouble, my brother and I saw that and didn't dare do that."

Yet her father's more westernized nature and relaxed rules also allowed Moni to flourish with autonomy. He took her to the market on his motorbike—they didn't have a car then—and showed her where to find supplies for the restaurant. The vendors, overcome with Moni's cuteness, would lean down, and pinch her pudgy, round cheeks and chirp, "Oh, you're so cute," and hand her extra chocolate and fruit. When the restaurant ran out of staples like rice, vegetables, steak meat, or the ingredients for the cakes and pies her father baked, he sent Moni off with a list and a pocketful of rupees. She pedaled her BMX bike frantically to the market fifteen minutes away, tied the items on her back, and with the same zeal, pedaled back to the kitchen, delivering the goods while beaming with pride. She was so small that her father fashioned a tall stool for her to sit on so she could watch him whip up desserts in the kitchen and make change for customers when he took a break. A German guest taught her father how to make apple strudel and lemon meringue pie and he would make extra for Moni and her siblings. Fresh out of the oven, he placed the deserts on a shelf to cool, the sweet scents wafting through the entire restaurant. Once, Moni heard whispers about a hashish cake and spotted one on the highest shelf that was off-limits to kids. Curious, she waited until the crumbs fell to the tray and nibbled at them to see what the fuss and secrecy was all about.

When Moni was upset with her mother for trying to make her cook or clean at home, or when she disliked the curry Shanti had prepared for dinner, she would dart out the door, sprint to the family restaurant, cozy up to the counter, and devour her favorite café food. Quietly, she instructed the staff not to tell her mum.

One day, her mother asked her to do the dishes.

"Today, yes, but only if brother does them tomorrow," Moni shot back.

"Only women do dishes," Shanti admonished.

Dirty dishes in hand, Moni sprang from the table to the kitchen sink and angrily scrubbed plates while plotting her next rebellion. From a young age, Moni loathed the gender disparities she witnessed inside and outside her family, especially the venerated strength and value of boys over girls.

When her brother came home late, no questions were asked, but for Moni or her sister, it was an inquisition: "Where were you? Who were you with?" her parents interrogated.

"Our blood is exactly the same," she asserted indignantly, rolling her big brown eyes and shrugging her shoulders.

As a teen, for neighborhood fun, she raced her male friends from campus to city center on her motorbike, easily beating them. They would line up at the campus gate, and the second it opened, charge through, barreling toward town. When they reassembled about fifteen minutes later, the loser bought ice cream. Her girlfriends called frequently, asking, "Ma timro bike ma aaouchu?" Please can I have a ride?

Moni's father promised to buy her a motorbike if she passed her exams with top marks, which was easy for her. But she was forbidden to ride on a motorbike with a boy. These restrictions infuriated Moni. She rode the bike all over Kathmandu, sometimes riding to dance parties dressed in a miniskirt, a big cultural taboo in the 1990s.

"Respectable Nepali girls wore traditional saris," Moni said. "Relatives start noticing properly dressed girls. They ask, 'Oh, whose girl is that in the beautiful sari?' And that's how arranged marriages start."

Nepali women who wore skirts were not considered good wife material, Moni explained.

"In our culture, a woman's body should not stand out or they are considered 'easy.' Most men and families looking for a wife would say they don't want that girl wearing a skirt—she's promiscuous, a rule breaker."

Moni's behavior became worrisome to her mother, who began to fret about her daughter's marriage prospects. Mohan was less concerned.

"Even though Moni had more freedom than most Newari girls, had been exposed to foreigners, rode a motor scooter, and most of her friends were boys, I trusted her," he said. "I would say to her, 'Mhya Macha, don't cut off your father's nose. If you make a mistake with boys, I can't show my face.'"

RULEBREAKER

Bangkok, Thailand 2003

Moni arrived by plane and loved the freedom she found. Tropical heat. The city buzz with its neon glow, street vendor clatter, chili pepper, burning charcoal, lemon-garlic-fumed food, the lime-mango-turquoise outfits of hawkers. The jumble of cultures and friendly people excited her. Most of all, she liked the freedom—an exceptional kind of freedom, the sort most Nepali women never have the opportunity to experience.

In those days, a single woman was not allowed to travel or stay one night away from home—not even to go camping—let alone travel or study internationally. But after rounds and rounds of arguments with her father, and months of pleading to study business abroad—to become as skilled a businessperson as her father—Moni wore him down and he relented. Cheerfully, she left for Assumption University in Bangkok, unaccompanied and loosely entrusted to distant relatives in Thailand.

Surprisingly, this is where her mountaineering obsession took root, or at least was brought to consciousness. Freshman year while drinking tea with a college friend, her friend asked about Mount Everest, its power and mystique. Despite Moni's history in the trekking business and a view of Everest from Kathmandu, her home city, she knew nothing about the famed mountain except that it proudly shot through the Himalayan sky of her country. Her friend ribbed Moni about her ignorance. Later that night, in her university hostel room, she couldn't sleep. Her Thai friend's words gnawed at her as childhood memories from the Himalaya's Guest House drifted back.

That spring, when she returned to Nepal for summer break, Moni watched *National Geographic* movies about Everest, absorbing every detail, determined to return to Thailand well-informed. In the fall, she returned to Assumption University knowledgeable about Mount Everest, but restless and mercurial. Less than two years into a Business Management program, she quit, returned to Kathmandu, and signed up for a mountaineering course.

When Moni announced that she was quitting school, her mother tried to talk her out of it, listing off the merits of completing a college degree, but Moni had made up her mind. Back in Kathmandu, she enrolled in a German class and signed up for an ABC training course, an outdoor leadership program for women sponsored by the Nepal Mountaineering Association (NMA). In the growing global economy, the NMA had instituted a program encouraging female leaders to work in the tourism and guiding industry. Moni was one of seventeen women accepted into the program.

Upon receiving this news, her parents grimaced in disapproval, her father, deeply disappointed that he had funded his daughter's education abroad and now it had abruptly ended, all that money gone to waste. And now that Moni was out of school with strings of unstructured days, her mother began hounding her again to marry. As customary in Newari culture, when a young woman comes of age or completes her education—usually by grade ten or twelve—her mother begins preparing her for the *magi-bihe*, arranged marriage. Moni's first marriage proposal came in tenth grade. She was fifteen. To her glee, her father rebuffed the proposal, having decided that she was too young and required an education first. But now, at nineteen, her mother had already begun consulting a lama and astrologers, casting about for a perfectly aligned match—not only a match suitable in caste and wealth, but also one in which the couple is destined to be joined based on previous lives. Her job of networking, negotiating, and collecting photographs was already done and she had lined up several prospective Newari husbands for Moni to choose from. In Newari tradition, once Moni chose a husband, a marriage proposal would come from the groom's family, and they would exchange flower garlands and gold rings. Moni's parents would offer her as a gift to the groom along with an agreed-upon dowry. Once an agreement was reached, the groom and the priest would find an auspicious date for marriage based on the lunar calendar.

Shanti approached her with photographs of eligible men—affluent engineers and doctors.

"Look, Moni," she said in Newari. "These men are from good families, are intelligent and well educated."

Furious, Moni pushed aside the photos, "I don't want to marry!"

To her parents' dismay, she left for the training in Pokhara. Her knowledge of mountaineering extended only so far as what she picked up in childhood, mainly from brief interactions with guests at her family's Himalaya's Guest House. She gleaned information from foreign tourists donning sunhats and neck scarves, swinging their colorful backpacks and walking sticks as they set off for the six-hour drive to Pokhara where they would begin a trek to Everest Basecamp or the Annapurna trek along the thirty-four-mile Annapurna Massif. They gushed about the beauty of the high-altitude route: the bamboo forests, traditional ethnic villages, and the awe-inspiring, snow-tipped Himalayas. They spoke in awe of the formidable Annapurna I, the tenth highest mountain (26,545 feet) and one of the world's deadliest to climb because of its extremely steep face that juts straight up 9,800 feet. They spieled off the names of the mountain peaks—Dhaulagiri, Machhapuchhre, Mansalu, Gangapurna, Tilicho Peak, Pisang Peak, Paungda Danda— mountains and names unfamiliar to Moni.

CHOOSE: BACKPACK OR HUSBAND?

2003 Bhaktapur Nepal

Flicking away photos of eligible men, and to her mother's dismay, Moni Mulepati chose a backpack instead of a husband. In the fall of 2003, she headed to the Annapurnas. Accessed from Pokhara Valley in north central Nepal, the thirty-four-mile-long Annapurna massif, named after the Hindu goddess of food and nourishment, lies between the Marsyangdi River and Kali Gandaki River, one of the deepest carved gorges in the world. Once, millions of years ago, this imposing belt of mountains—thirty in all—sat at the bottom of a warm Teyths Sea before being pushed up by colliding plates. Now, this ridge of pyramid-shaped peaks soars 19,000 feet into the sky. Their arresting beauty makes the Annapurna one of the most renowned trekking routes in Nepal. The landscape is majestic, with snowcapped peaks, terraced farmland, stone house villages, and lush forests and meadows. Even the barren, wind-swept terrain scourged by the forces of nature is exquisitely beautiful.

Moni stuffed her newly purchased backpack with blue jeans and other daily clothes and toiletries as if she were packing for vacation, stood up, took a few awkward steps forward, and nearly toppled over. When she arrived at the training course and met up with the sixteen other women, she noticed that their packs were leaner, more manageable.

A few days into the fifteen-day training, after lugging her hulking pack around camp with a lot of grumbling, Moni flung it to the ground and angrily proclaimed, "This is not for me." City life seemed far superior to her in the moment.

"You'll need that pack tomorrow, too," her teacher scolded, pointing at Moni's backpack. Later, another leader would single her out and encourage her, saying, "I know you are strong and can do this, Moni."

Moni dug in, finished the outdoor training course, and learned the basics of outdoor living—safety, communication, first aid, navigation, leadership, and responsibility. At the end of the course, she gave the keynote address, and, at the urging of her instructors, signed up for Basic Mountaineering. Moni returned home from the ten-day training course that went from Pokhara to Ghandruk to Annapurna Basecamp energized by the experience, power, and camaraderie, and the encouragement of her trainer, Nimi Sherpa, who recognized Moni's adventuresome spirit. Nimi awarded Moni best participant and encouraged her to take two more courses, Basic and Advanced Mountaineering. A week later, Moni was applying to Basic Training.

Moni arrived home from Pokhara cheerful and with a sense of accomplishment. She was at the computer typing an email to her friends when her mother entered the room and handed her a photograph.

"He's a good family guy, is intelligent and well educated," she began, before Moni interrupted.

"I dislike this guy," Moni said, shoving the photo away. "I don't want to marry and I don't care about rich men. I am applying to mountaineering training," she announced.

"You just got back from Pokhara," her mother said. "Climbing is dreadful. Why are you doing this, Moni? I told you to complete your courses in Bangkok, but you just wasted this time."

"Daddy already agreed on it," Moni told her mother, shaking her head obstinately.

Her mother fumed. "Oh God, how did my daughter get this way?" she sputtered, leaving the room.

After completing Basic Mountaineering, Moni signed up for the Advanced Mountaineering course, where she would train at Everest Basecamp and the foot of the Khumbu Icefall. Once she paid for the course, her excitement grew.

"I got really excited when I heard the sound of Everest, but Khumbu Icefall? What's that? I knew nothing about it."

Only four of the sixteen women who completed the previous courses would be selected for advanced training, and Moni was chosen to move ahead. She had heard that completing the advanced course would open more doors for her, and although she had no clear sense of what she wanted to do—other than not marry—if it was not business school or becoming a pilot, it was mountaineering.

Meanwhile, back in Kathmandu, her parents, still aggravated with the mountaineering track, began to enlighten her about the Newari path. With a degree of frustration, they contended that the Advanced Training Course was her last.

"No more money," they declared.

It was time she attended cooking classes and accepted a marriage proposal.

THE COURTSHIP

December 2003 – January 2004
Langtang, Nepal

On a chilly day in December, Pem hopped on a bus in Kathmandu and made the seven-hour journey to Syabru Besi along with thirty other students.

"The Syabru Besi is about 16,400 feet, a Grand Teton type-mountain," Pem said.

The group trekked through small villages perched on the riverside, rhododendron forests, a few teahouses, and stone homes. As an interesting aside, Pem tells the story of how a Sherpa from Namche and Kumjing became the chief ranger of Syabru Besi National Park and implemented a rule that hotels in the park could only have six bedrooms. Now, these hotels cannot expand. The king did not make the same rule for Namche, which allowed the village to receive the bulk of tourism.

The next morning, the group trekked another two days to Langtang Village and Yala Peak Basecamp where they would begin a month-long advanced course in mountaineering. On the bus, Pem sat behind Moni, but she didn't notice him.

Yala Peak rises 18,000 feet above Nepal's Langtang Valley near the Tibetan border. The valley, a landscape of hanging glaciers, hemlock forests, and moraines, is set against a backdrop of snowy Himalayan peaks that tower above Tamang's hillside settlements where farmers and yak herders tend to their crops and herds. The fluted peak of Ganchenpo Mountain in the Jugal Range rises gracefully into the blue sky, the tall peaks of Tibet hanging right behind it. The trekking path to Yala Peak was on an old trade route passing through land of the Tamang, descendants of Tibetans. On the route, Pem passed stone houses and children on bicycles, women winnowing rice after harvest, the Kyanjin Gompa monastery, yak herders, and the Trisuli and Bhote Losi rivers. In 2015, a decade after Pem and Moni had trained at Yala Peak, the beautiful landscape valley was decimated when hanging glaciers broke off in an earthquake and wiped out the entire village.

Yala Peak is a non-technical climb, its gradual ascent offering a stable place to practice advanced mountaineering skills like roping up in a group, clipping in, line safety and pacing, scrambling on loose rock, walking in crampons, and self-arrest—using an ice axe as a brake to stop a fall down a snow slope. The Yala Peak training program was a government initiative designed to produce more mountain guides in Nepal, especially women, and a perfect place to build on the basic mountaineering skills Pem had learned in Manang, and Moni in the Anapurna.

Moni Mulepati first stepped into Pem Sherpa's view wearing a black miniskirt, tall black boots, and fashionable glasses, her mane of silky jet-black hair cascading down her back. She was an elegant contrast to the other Nepali women dressed in drab, fleecy, loose-fitting climbing garb.

"To a village boy like me, she looked like a movie star," Pem said.

While waiting for her interview for the Advanced Mountaineering course, Moni walked to the front of the registration line with a high, bouncy stride, one hand on her hip, the other tapping the shoulders of acquaintances she had met at previous trainings.

"Oh, hello, how are you? Good seeing you..." she chattered away, gesturing warmly.

Everyone noticed her. Her toned, amber skin, round girlish face and angular cheekbones, generous lips, and striking brown eyes gazed sharply back as she conversed. Moni sat down on a bench in the corner of the interview room next to a collection of climbing equipment and posters and began talking to another Nepali girl.

"So..." Moni chirped, twirling her hair with her fingers.

That's when Pem noticed her. He scanned her from head to toe, astonished. Clearly not from the village, he thought, wondering if this exceptionally pretty, fashionable city girl with vermillion-painted nails and a broad, white-toothed smile was enrolling in the mountaineering training program for Mount Everest guiding. Mount Everest! Dubious, he eyed Moni and the small group of women surrounding her and tried to puzzle out the incongruency before him.

"I ask myself, are these girls really doing climbing training for a living? Then, I actually ask this question to the teacher giving the Advanced Mountaineering registration interview!" Pem said.

The interviewer called out the next name on his list—"Miss Moni Mulepati"—and the pretty woman in the skirt stood up from the bench and walked upstairs to the interview room, her heels clacking against the floor.

Incredulous, Pem repeated her name under his breath, and wondered privately, *The lady who wears skirt—can she climb Everest Mountain?*

Since running away from Chyangba to work in Namche, and on the heels of completing a French-sponsored First Aid course for mountaineers, Pem had become serious-minded about mountaineering, intensely focused on becoming a guide in France. He held little tolerance for flighty girls, or anyone, for that matter, who trivialized the profession and dangers of Everest mountaineering.

Sure enough, smack dab in the heart of a Kathmandu winter, dressed in a miniskirt and high-heel boots as she stood in line with a group of Nepalis—mostly men—Moni Mulepati was, *unmistakably,* enrolled in Advanced Mountaineering Training for guiding at Mount Everest. Moni, along with three other Nepali women and twenty-six men from the Sherpa, Gurung, and Rai castes had passed the written and oral exams and were accepted as trainees.

At first, Pem found Moni to be a bit of a distraction, but he remained quiet and focused on his goal of becoming an international guide, separating himself from the thirty other trainees by training alone, for the most part.

Moni first noticed Pem while rock climbing at Balaju. She was talking to Phula Sherpa about where she could find a pair of climbing boots that would fit her small feet. Phula mentioned that his cousin might have a pair at home.

"Who is your cousin?" Moni asked.

Phula pointed to the rock wall. Moni looked up to see Pem stemming across the rock practicing handholds. *He has very nice hair,* she thought to herself.

Their first night of training, Moni seethed with irritation. After retiring to bed in a shared room with her friend Dolma Sherpa, she couldn't sleep. The men's voices from downstairs carried up through the thin floors and kept her awake. She recognized Pem and Phula's voices talking foolish boy talk about eating rice and beans and digestion issues, driving motorbikes on the ring road, crashing into trees, a motorbike falling into the river, wounds and torn pants. Tired of the loud nonsense, Moni rose from bed, and, not caring if she woke her roommate, began stomping on the floor to shush them.

The men stopped talking and listened.

"Who the heck is that?" Pem asked, looking at Phula.

"Me!" Moni shouted angrily through the floorboards. "I'm disturbed listening to you chatting nonsense."

Pem looked up and spoke directly to the ceiling, "Put cotton in your ears, then, and sleep."

Phula and Pem looked at each other, laughed, and resumed their rowdy conversation.

Above, Moni banged wildly on her bedroom floor again, sending a blast of dust, bamboo splinters, and ire down on them. To her, nothing about this was funny.

"Dumb boys," she thought out loud. "Especially Pem, the one who doesn't talk except loudly at night when others are trying to sleep."

For Moni, it was not love at first sight. Her first sense of Pem registered as deep irritation that would stick like a burr for quite some time.

In the high mountains, Pem was a fast climber compared to the other trainees, often the first to arrive at the summit or destination. But during Yala Peak training, his pace slowed. He would stop and sit on a boulder listening to his MP3, secretly watching for Moni, wondering how far back she was, how she was coping with the steep, hilly terrain.

Once, early on in the training course, Dolma Sherpa passed Pem on the trail where he was resting, and asked, "Pem Dorjee, how could you walk up so much faster in these hilly trails?"

"Maybe I'm being a Sherpa," he joked.

"But I am Sherpa too, and I couldn't climb this hilly trail as fast as you," Dolma grumbled as she stood on the side of the trail gulping water and catching her breath.

"It may be the lack of energy in your body," Pem teased. "Have full stomach of rice and meat like I do, then you can climb up the hilly trails like me!" Dolma nodded and smiled and continued up the hill just as Moni rounded a switchback. Pem sat on the boulder waiting, eager to talk, but when she reached him, all that squeaked out of his mouth was "hello."

Moni stopped in the middle of the trail, and, arms crossed, said tersely, "Hello. Please give me your stick."

Pem handed over his walking stick, painfully searching for words, but too shy to speak. Not stopping to rest, Moni continued uphill leaving Pem sitting tongue-tied on the stone. He shoved his water bottle into his rucksack, pulling it closer to his side preparing to jump up and walk with Moni, but hesitated and instead put his Walkman on and watched her until she disappeared. He sat on the stone waiting for his friends further down the mountain.

At dinner, Moni handed the walking stick back to Pem and scanned the dining table for a seat. Pem gestured to an open chair next to him, but Moni, her face averted, jaw fixed, the fine shape of her head already bobbing in conversation, sat next to Phula. Pem watched Phula and other trainees talking with Moni, stealing glances when she wasn't looking, then sat down next to Phula. He quietly observed Moni while trying to work up the courage to talk.

Moni and the other three female trainees ended up sitting together at dinner regularly with the men dispersing around them. When the girls asked for a second serving of food, the men swooped in like vultures and hung around. Second helpings were dished out only to the women, leaving the hungry boys to curry favor with the girls—offering to carry their backpacks or handing over extra chocolate, tea, or batteries from their packs—in exchange for an extra scoop of eggs, dal bhat, boiled potatoes. The girls affectionately named these hungry men "Tanker" because they ate so much.

The server lined up the rice, dal, meat, pickle, and eggs on the table and placed a bowl of boiled potatoes in front of Moni.

Pem glanced at Moni, surprised by the large bowl of potatoes in front of her. "I think you very much like boiled potatoes, am I right?"

"I like it," Moni replied. "I don't like meat. I am satisfied with these boiled potatoes," she said, as she bit into a skinless potato with pickle.

Still annoyed with Pem for keeping her awake, Moni refused to sit next to him and did her best to ignore him. To draw her in, Pem tried a different tact. He offered her a few CDs from his music collection to listen to as she climbed. And, in the dining hall, he began talking about his mountaineering experiences and trainings with Dolma and the other two girls.

His voice, loud and filled with bravado, whirled around the dining room:

> *"First, I took the guide training at Ravi Bhawan orga-nized by the Nepal Ministry of Tourism. It was a forty-five-day long training, and we were trained on different mountains of Nepal in mountaineering, biodiversity, and first aid," he bragged. "Then I participated in basic mountaineering training in Manang organized by the Nepal Mountain Association for thirty days."*

He turned and snuck a peek at Moni to see if he had her attention. Although still sitting with her back to him, he could tell she was listening.

"There was an incident in Manang," Pem said mysteriously.

"What happened?" Dolma asked.

Curious now, Moni got up and sat quietly in front of Dolma and closer to Pem as he told his story.

> *A friend and I climbed the training peak that day, but when we came back down, my friend lost his $200 sunglasses given to him by a client. It was dark, so I say we should come back in morning because we are not allowed to leave camp at night. But we went back up and have to stay at Manang for the night after we looked for the glasses. It was too late to get back to Humde which was a little far from Manang. The rules of the mountaineering school were that we could not leave Humde.*

> *When we returned, an action of discipline was taken against us because we stayed at Manang and broke the*

rules. I was not allowed to take part in any training.
Still, my friend wrote a letter and sent it to Nepal
Mountaineering Association asking them to change the
penalty decision and they reduced it to one year. They
said only after a year could I participate. So, I stayed
in Kathmandu doing nothing for a year. If I was not
in punishment, I would have finished this training last
year. It's nothing bad, though. It is best that I was in
punishment.

Pem smiled at Moni when he finished his story.

"It was best that you were punished?" Moni asked, puzzled, suddenly feeling uneasy for dropping her guard and speaking to Pem directly.

Boldly, in front of everyone and looking directly at Moni, Pem said, "I'm participating in this training a year later just so I can meet Moni! Right? Otherwise, how would I meet her?"

Those were daring words for a shy young man like Pem. As he would soon discover, Moni Mulepati's stunning beauty and unabashed style was not all that set her apart. In the coming months and years, before his eyes and the entire country of Nepal, a star would unfold—a woman who dreamed bold and bright, who dared to forge her own identity by defying the deep-rooted traditions of the culture she was born into, a culture of obedience and subjugation of women—and do so with such fierceness that it was hard to hold on to. He would discover too, that, like him, Moni was an outlier, aching to bust out.

By the time they reached Yala Peak summit, Pem and Moni were close. The training groups were determined by speed and experience. Pem placed in the faster section. He met Moni and her group on their way down from the summit.

"By the time Moni's group had reached camp, they were so tired, they couldn't even take off their shoes," Pem said, laughing.

In her own defense, Moni chimed in, "Michiri was crying and had a blister. Guys were bringing her hot water, including Pem," she said, a trace of both rivalry and satisfaction in her voice.

In fact, from the flirtations she observed between Pem and Michiri—Michiri sitting on Pem's back while he did push-ups—Moni thought the two were a couple.

"I was just trying to make Moni jealous," Pem chided. "She needs negative fire to get her going."

By the end of the advanced training course, Pem and Moni had forged a friendship and romance that would drastically alter the course and shape of their lives. But first, Sagarmatha called Pem. His first summit bid.

EXPEDITION PLAN
THE GAMBLE

May 2004

"*T imi yo garna sakchou, Moni, malai thacha timi yo garna sakchou. You know, Moni, I think you can do this,*" Pem said haltingly, huffing for breath as he stood at the top of Sagarmatha looking down over the Tibetan Plateau and an expanse of bone-white clouds and snowy peaks, his satellite phone pressed to his ear. Moni was climbing Island Peak (20,305 feet) when Pem called. She listened closely, lured by his words, and to her surprise, with more certainty than struggle, she began imagining her own possibility of summiting Everest.

It was a bold, cosmic, and slightly impossible dream Pem envisioned, a dream that had grown imperceptibly across his young adulthood, enlarging like the inside space of a heart. As he confronted one obstacle after another, his heart opened and shut and opened again, each obstacle, each decision a negotiation between economic benefit and a high risk of death. Through it all, his trust in the crystal blue Himalayan horizon he had set his sights on never wavered, although his dream of living abroad as a mountain guide had shifted to make room for love.

He imagined a second summit expedition, this time, an all-Nepali team that included Moni. He and Moni would elope at the summit if they made it, setting new records that would generate enough buzz and notoriety to improve their chances of emigrating from Nepal. If successful, Moni would be the first Newari woman to summit and they would be the first couple to marry at the top of the world, with the added twist of breaking Nepali caste tradition that forbade a marriage between a Sherpa and Newari. If their team could pull it off, Pem fully believed that his marriage to Moni on Everest's summit would skitter across national news and sharply recast their lives. Yet, he also understood that the formidable circumstances came with a huge risk of failure. To begin with, Sagarmatha's cosmos would have to square: the mountain protector deities and local spirits had to be properly influenced and pleased. Gods willing, in addition, the weather had to cooperate, their bodies and cognition hold up under Everest's extremes, and no accident-causing mistakes strike the team. And still, a cutting question remained. Would their families approve of their marriage after the fact, or would one or both be exiled, their families torn apart and shamed? What would they do if their families didn't agree to the marriage? Would their love survive?

It was a strategic time to lead an all-Nepali team to Everest, Pem realized. The timing couldn't be better, with government-sponsored programs in effect encouraging women to enter the mountaineering profession. That, combined with Pem's recent Everest summit and Moni's achievement of the highest level of mountaineering training, set the stage. They both believed that a successful summit would bring opportunities and open doors that had remained closed to them due to class, geography, gender, and circumstance.

In May 2004, immediately after Pem summited, he and Moni began to develop an expedition plan, explore potential team members, and kick around ideas for organizing sponsorship and fundraising. The biggest hurdle they faced was how to bring Moni's parents on board while keeping their relationship and plans to elope secret. They saw each other frequently, taking morning walks together at Swayambhu and going on training hikes. In the seclusion of the wooded trails, they walked hand in hand. When tired, they dropped their packs to the ground and laid in the snow, Moni resting her head on Pem's shoulder as he put his hand on her head, pulling her close.

To maintain control and a high-profile leadership position, their expedition would be small. Small team, small budget, no porters. The risk and success would be their own. Their team, they decided, would comprise three members: Pem, Moni, and Kami Sherpa, Pem's cousin who had summited Everest the previous year with Peak Promotion. This would be Kami's fourth summit attempt, and his valuable experience would contribute significantly to the team's success.

Kami was raised in a small village about an hour and a half walk from Chyangba. Like Pem, he came from a family of mostly farmers who raised vegetables and barley. Although Kami and Pem didn't know each other very well growing up, they later became good friends and roommates in Kathmandu, where they shared an apartment. Although Kami's parents never encouraged him to have a life outside the village, as a kid, he developed ambitions.

"My dream was to climb all the mountains I could see from the village, but I didn't know how," he said.

An opportunity for Kami to leave the village came when his uncle, renowned mountaineer Wongchu Sherpa, convinced Kami's mother to send him to Kathmandu to learn English. Wongchu was living in Kathmandu at the time and could look in on his nephew. After time spent learning English, Kami found work as a dishwasher for an expedition company operating at Everest Basecamp and worked his way into a climbing position. He reached the summit in 1997, a year after the 1996 Everest tragedy. His first summit as a climbing Sherpa came in 2002, while working for Peak Promotion. As a member of David Breashears' film crew that included renowned professional climber Jimmy Chin, Kami carried and set up equipment on the mountain. It was a scary job at times, he said.

"The wind is so cold and strong and the snow flies around and you can't see anything. Sometimes you get lifted off the ground or pushed over by the wind."

For safety, film crew members were clipped into a safety rope, but on the worst weather days, in high winds and minus forty-degree Fahrenheit temperatures, the work was unnerving.

Kami is a small man, barely 5 feet tall and 140 pounds, his whole frame thin, almost as if undernourished. His face is narrow, his skin smooth with a slight weathered look and the beginning of crow's feet around his eyes. Kami is painfully shy or deferential, his glance often cast down, especially when speaking with someone or when complimented on his achievements.

To leverage the prestige of their expedition team and set them apart from other teams, Moni was designated expedition leader. Hopefully, she would become the first Newari female to stand on Everest. To train, Pem took Moni to practice climbing skills on smaller, less threatening mountains—Phulchoki, Champadevi, Shivapuri, Nagarjun, Jamacho—where they conditioned by carrying heavy loads up and down the mountain. Moni found the training difficult. Once, at the Mulepati home, while she, Kami, and her mother were watching a video of Kami summiting Everest, Moni confided in Kami that she was angry with Pem for making her carry such a heavy rucksack while training at Yala and Island Peaks. Kami encouraged her, but at the same time, gently tried to prepare Moni for Everest without scaring her or her mother.

"We won't have porters. Remember, Moni, the altitude is much higher at Everest. It's a harder climb than Yala Peak."

As they watched the video, Kami began to itemize the gear required to reach the summit: food, drinking water, juice, tent, sleeping pad, ice ax, climbing gear...

"The oxygen cylinders weigh six to fifteen pounds each," he said, continuing the list.

Shanti interrupted, "Kami, did you feel any difficulties breathing in the high altitude?" she asked.

"It's not so difficult," he said. "I need oxygen only after Camp IV. It depends on your respiration technique."

When the video ended, Moni took Kami up to the seventh-floor veranda garden. Designed and planted by her father, the garden was a lush refuge from the busyness of the city, densely filled with trees, shrubs, flowers, vegetables, and a water fountain. Moni loved the garden, the sweet rose and jasmine scents, the colorful orange and pinks in the bird of paradise, the cucumbers. The housemaid had cut up kitchen scraps and Moni tossed them in the compost with the worms and mixed it with her bare hands. Some of the garden plants were used for healing. Moni's grandfather, Mohan's father, was a popular healer and didn't believe in doctors. He had hoped a son would take over his healing practice and tried to inspire Mohan, but "it didn't take," Moni said, "Dad couldn't get the knowledge."

As Kami was leaving, Moni's father, Mohan, walked in. He was returning from a health checkup for his heart problems, and the three spoke for a minute before going to bed.

Energized from Kami's video of climbing Everest and their conversation, Moni began looking through her Advanced Training course packet and the packing lists. On the long list of first aid items was a Gamow Bag, a portable inflatable hyperbaric bag used to counter the effects of high-altitude sickness. A Gamow Bag simulates a descent—the safest way to aid recovery—but in cases where descent is not possible or advisable due to weather, a dangerous situation exists, the climber is unable to move on their own, or there is a lack of rescuers available, the Gamow Bag can be effective. Hypoxic climbers are zipped into the pressurized body-sized bag that is pumped with fresh air that quickly fills their lungs with much-needed oxygen. If climbing Everest was in her future, Moni thought, "I hope we don't have to use this ever."

She read on. *Mountaineers must carry a topo map, compass, pencil and paper, altimeter,* followed by a long equipment list, most of the items she would have to purchase:

- Crampons
- Belay
- Rock Hammer
- Jumar
- Summit suit
- Gate Opening
- Ice ax
- Rock piton
- Dead Man anchor
- Figure Eight
- Harness
- Climbing sling
- UV filter
- Helmet
- Snow bar
- Screw gate
- Carabiner

She read on to a troubling list of problems, diseases, and available treatments—*if any*:

- AMS Acute Mountain Sickness
- HAPE – High Altitude Pulmonary Edema

- HACE – High Altitude Cerebral Edema
- Frostbite
- Snow blindness
- Hypothermia
- Diarrhea
- Vomiting
- Pain in legs
- Indigestion
- Sunburn
- No alcohol, smoking, sleeping pills
- Drink 3-4 liters of water per day

Moni set the Advanced Training course packet aside and went upstairs. She picked up one of several Everest magazines that Pem had given her and was immediately captivated by the stories of the first women to summit—Junko Tabei (Japan 1975), Phanthog (Tibet, 1975), Wanda Rutkiewicz (Poland 1978), and Pasang Lhamu Sherpa, the thirty-two-year-old wife, mother and businesswoman who summited Everest in April 1993, but died while descending, and Lhakpa Sherpa who, in 2005, was attempting a fifth summit from the North side. Moni stepped out onto the veranda, deep in thought, and watched her father fill a flower box with soil and carefully lay in new flowering plants, watering their roots.

"Daddy," Moni began hopefully, "Pem and Kami *dai*," she said, using a Newari term of endearment, "they will help me with the Everest expedition. I'm working hard, training, and hiking. How could we manage to find more money?"

Her father laughed. "I'll discuss sponsorship with my friends at the Rotary," he said.

For years, Mohan Mulepati had been a charter member of the Rotary Club of New Road City in Kathmandu, where he had a strong network of friends. In 2004, at a Rotary meeting, charter members announced that in 2005, they planned to send three climbers on an expedition to Everest in celebration of Rotary International's centennial.

"If you sponsor me, I'll climb," Moni playfully bantered with her father.

But beneath the playfulness was a daughter driven to climb Everest. Elated, Moni took her father's response to take it up with the Rotarians as a "yes." With one arrow in her quiver, she felt adequately armed to convince her mother. But soon, she would realize that it would take time to bring her mother around. In the meantime, Moni acted as if she was already on what would become the Rotary Nepal Centennial Everest Expedition team, or Rotary team, and continued training. She became the charter president of the Rotaract Club of New Road City, Kathmandu, and began working with the nine committee members on fundraising.

As Moni was filling out a form for the Advanced Training mountaineering class, Shanti entered the room, gently put her arm on her daughter's shoulder, and handed her a photograph. Moni glanced at it quickly.

"A good family," her mother chirped. "He's intelligent and well educated," she began, but Moni interrupted.

"I dislike this guy. Please take this photo and don't talk about this matter now," she snapped, handing back the photograph.

Shanti argued with Moni again, repeating her objections to her climbing interests.

"Climbing a mountain is very difficult and dreadful, too. Why are you going on this track?" she asked angrily. "I told you many times to go and complete the course in Bangkok. You wasted it, completing only one and half years," she scolded. "You already trekked to Annapurna Base Camp. That's enough. Don't go to the mountaineering training. You need to marry."

"I'm not interested in marrying now," Moni said. "Besides, Daddy already agreed on me taking this course and maybe climbing Everest."

"God, why? How did I get a daughter like this?" her mother sputtered, storming from the room.

Wanting to keep the peace, Moni softened and sought out her mother, who was puttering in an adjacent room, and promised that she would choose a husband once she had met her mountaineering goal of summiting Everest.

PART III

ROTARY NEPAL CENTENNIAL
EVEREST EXPEDITION 2005

March 28 – May 31, 2005 (64 days)

Everest Basecamp 2005 Rotary Nepal Centennial Everest Expedition Team
Altitude: 18,000 ft / 5,486 m
Average Temperature: minus 40 degrees F
Wind: 65 mph
Pem Dorjee Sherpa, Team Member (right)
Moni Sherpa, Expedition Leader (middle)
Kami Sherpa, Team Member (left)

Sagun Puja
March 28, 2005

At 5 a.m., about the time the sun begins to rise over the Tibetan Plateau, its soft yellow glow close to the valley floor and visible from Everest's summit, Pem, Moni, and Kami rose and began packing for their Everest expedition. They packed with strict practicality to avoid carrying extra weight up the mountain and checked their gear against a packing list to be sure they had crucial supplies: down summit suit, glacier glasses, goggles, climbing boots, gloves, mitts, hats, neck gaiters, sunscreen, harness, ascender, slings, carabiners, alpine ice axe, helmet, crampons, down sleeping bag and pad, thermal layers, headlamp, water bottles, thermos, water purification system, eating utensils, batteries, camera, watch, cutting tool, iPad with downloaded movies, camp stoves, phone, medication. The night before, when no one was around, Pem stuffed a few special items deep in his pack—a surprise to break out at the summit if the team made it.

Shanti rose early, too, busying herself with preparations for the farewell puja. She filled a copper butter lamp with rice and refreshed each bowl of holy water—one copper bowl for Newari tradition and seven for the Sherpa tradition. It was only proper to honor and bless her Newari daughter and two Sherpa climbing partners, blending traditions and cultures. She lit candles and incense, closed her eyes, and ran her smooth, slender hands gently through the trail of smoke rising over Ganesh, sweeping the incense toward her as she prayed.

Shanti is exceptionally beautiful. Her face is round, but angular around her cheekbones, giving her an exotic look, and her mouth is slightly turned down. At home, she wears her hair in a casual bun that rests neatly on the top of her spine as she moves around the house carefully, her sari swirling below her knees. Her expression is often subdued—almost with a look of worry or sadness—but when she breaks into a smile, her eyes light up, her face glowing with radiance and warmth.

Shanti, like her husband, comes from a prominent, entrepreneurial family with deep roots in Bhaktapur, Nepal. For generations, her family ran a prosperous chain of grocery stores and owned a fair amount of property. Shanti was one of seven children. Her mother gave birth to four daughters and three sons, though all her boys died young from various childhood illnesses. Her father took another wife to produce a male heir.

Following Newari tradition, Shanti's marriage to Mohan Mulepati was arranged and carried a dowry. Tucked between the pages of the Mulepati family photo album is Shanti's dowry record. Written on a long sheet of brown paper in curling Nepali scrawl, the dowry itemizes the gifts she brought to the match: dishes, 1 flower vase, 1 photo frame, 2 clocks, a pitcher, glasses... The items, saved over time and multiple moves, are scattered throughout the Mulepati home.

When it was time for the puja to begin, Shanti gathered family, friends, Pem, and Kami, and directed everyone to their places. Rice, betel nuts, money, and prayers were offered before Ganesh to remove any obstacles to the team's safe and successful Everest ascent. *Sagun* is an old and respected puja ceremony in the Newari community of the Kathmandu region where participants humbly pray for an individual's good luck and prosperity. The Sagun and its specific set of prayers is held during special life occasions such as a baby showers, birthdays and weddings, and to those setting off on a long journey or returning home.

Shanti leaned in and placed a red *tika* on everyone's forehead. Bows were made to elders, beginning with the oldest present, before food was received—a boiled egg, fish, *moon dahl* (a round flat bread), garlic, ginger. Moni received the food in her right hand, alcohol in her left, then bowed and took a bite of boiled egg followed by a sip of alcohol, then a bite of fish and another sip of alcohol. Gifts were presented to the team, mostly fruits and snacks—offerings and blessings for the team's safety. The puja ended with the clear ring of a bell, and everyone filed out of the room following traditional protocol.

"When leaving a Sagun, no one should call you from behind," Moni said. "It's bad luck."

After the puja, Moni, Pem, and Kami signed the Rotary Nepal Centennial Expedition agreement, gathered their backpacks, and drove to the Tribhuvan International airport in Kathmandu, leaving behind the safety and comfort of the lower Kathmandu Valley for the next few months.

There is no road equipped for car or bus travel between Kathmandu and Lukla, only a hiking trail, so rather than hike a few extra days, climbers take the thirty-minute flight to Lukla in a small plane or helicopter. Moni's family followed the team to the airport for a final, emotional farewell. When the team arrived, the Nepal TV crew was already interviewing Sherpas on their way to Everest. As she said goodbye to her family, Moni and her mother hugged and wept openly. The reality of what she was about to do set in, and Moni burst into tears. *What if this is last time I will see my family?* she thought.

"I worried I might die," she said. "Accidents happen. Or I might not return in one piece."

As the possibility of losing her daughter sank into Shanti's bones, she cried harder. Mohan, with perfect composure, gently pulled his wife close and soothed her.

"Father and daughter planned the Nepal Rotary team and expedition," he said softly. "We have Pem who has training and has been to Everest, and Kami has been to Everest many times," he reassured his wife. "The Rotary Nepal Expedition is a big opportunity to carry our flag to top of Everest."

In his own mind, they had soundly planned the expedition and with what little second-hand knowledge he had of climbing Everest, he was confident enough to send his daughter off without worry or regret.

Moni gave each family member a final hug and cleared her head quickly. She'd had a fair amount of practice with that since beginning her quest to be the first Newari woman to reach Everest's summit. She'd gotten past the ugly tricks of one competitor who tried to sabotage her expedition, and avoided being psyched out by a well-meaning friend who handed her a copy of Jon Krakauer's *Into Thin Air,* suggesting she read about the risks of Everest a few days before leaving. Moni politely thanked her for the gift, but in private, quickly tucked the book in a drawer.

"I refused to even look at the book," she said. Moni was ready for Everest.

The team scrambled to raise the $50,000 required to launch a three-member Everest expedition team.

"We were running back and forth trying to get sponsors," Moni said.

It's expensive to climb Everest. The permit alone was $10,000 per person. A good, lightweight down summit suit was another $10,000. They would opt for the heavier $200 Nepali-made version.

They had met the requirement, but in a discouraging setback, the Nepal Rotary reduced the team's sponsorship commitment, claiming budget shortfalls. Everyone behind the team used their connections to make up for the unexpected shortfall. The team sold raffle tickets, spoke at Rotaries across Nepal, and went from shop to shop asking for money or a specific donation—an oxygen bottle, a down summit suit, gloves, a case of Pringles, a permit fee waiver. A few days before departing for Everest, the team had once again met the $50,000 minimum, but their fundraising efforts were not over. Thanks to a very large sponsorship from Canon ($100,000), the team agreed that they would pay back any borrowed money. But there was a catch to the sponsorship. To collect the funds, the Rotary team had to take photos from the summit with a Canon camera provided by the company. Pem was confident the team would reach the summit, but without the $100,000 in the bank, Moni felt it prudent and ethical to exclude that cash from the total funds raised.

"If our team failed, how would I face my sponsors—my family and friends and even those who gave five dollars—and convince them that I wasn't running away with the money or I hadn't tried hard enough?" she said. "I was more worried about the trip being cancelled because of a cash shortage than of dying on Everest!"

The team would have to scrimp. Their expedition would be bare bones, with little room for extras and no extravagances. The three team members would do everything on their own—even cook for themselves if they had to. The team would navigate, manage their health, watch the weather, set up Basecamp, Camps II, III and IV, carry all their gear (50 to 70-pound packs), supplies, food, water, fuel, and oxygen tanks up the mountain without the support of guides or porters. Moni, Pem, and Kami accepted that doing all this work themselves would compromise their crucial energy supply, which could cost the team the summit—and worse, increase their risk of injury or death. To make the summit, they would have to plan wisely.

*　　*　　*

Sending a team to Everest in the spring of 2005 was a strategic decision by the Nepal Rotarians in Kathmandu. The expedition coincided with a prestigious Rotary International centennial event to be held in Chicago, the Rotary's birthplace. The lavish gala would take place in late June 2005 after the spring climbing season and would include Rotarians, speakers, and dignitaries from around the world. Back then, the Nepal Rotary was under the umbrella of India's Rotary district. All Rotarian business was conducted in Calcutta, an inconvenience, and a bit of an affront to Nepal. The Mulepati family had been long-standing Rotary members and were in favor of the expedition. If the Rotary Nepal Centennial Everest Expedition team successfully flew its flag at the summit, the publicity would put Nepal on the world stage and likely bring Kathmandu its own Rotary district.

Another strategic decision was to send Moni Mulepati to the summit and designate her the expedition team leader. At the time, the Nepali government and Bureau of Tourism were encouraging women to enter the Everest trekking and guiding profession, offering training programs to qualifying female applicants. If Moni reached the summit, Nepal would gain more notoriety as she would become the first Newari woman to summit Everest—that is, if she beat out one other Newari climber.

As expedition leader, one of Moni's primary responsibilities was to fundraise, a daunting task, she discovered. For two months, she had knocked on doors and gotten nowhere. Securing sponsorship with the same ease as foreigners seemed impossible. During a meeting with the Core Rotary Committee, the members offered her a piece of advice.

"Change your get up," they said. "Look like a Sherpa and wear backpacking gear. People will take you more seriously."

Stunned, Moni had frowned and shaken her head in dismay. Even the gym trainer where Moni and her team trained for Everest didn't take her seriously. When she told him that she didn't want to bulk up and have big arms like the men, he thought she was lazy. He took Pem aside and told him that Moni would never climb. Later, Pem divulged the insult to Moni, knowing it would motivate her.

Skeptical and disillusioned, yet determined, Moni swapped out her Newari city fashion—stylish skirts and high boots—for mountaineering gear and a rucksack. Suddenly, the dollars poured in.

As she dedicated her time to raising money, Moni would discover that some climbers saw themselves as competitors rather than comrades. To achieve the summit, she would have to learn to temper her frustrations and negative emotions, especially when it came to her main competitor, another Newari woman chasing the same goal.

Her nemesis, Michiri, was also a novice mountaineer and had attended the same mountaineering training program as Moni. Because of her gossipy, dramatic ways, someone at Basecamp nicknamed her "Michiri" after the Lamas who perform in the spring Dumji festival dressed in costume and masked faces.

Michiri was assertive and carried a sense of advantage as naturally as breath. She was dark-haired and petite, possessed a kind of earthy natural beauty and a breezy, willowy walk that exuded the kind of confidence and sexual availability that turned men's heads. Moni didn't trust her.

Moni's instincts that Michiri was untrustworthy were right. Early in the fundraising stage Michiri tried to sabotage their expedition. Moni had secured several large sponsors which would have funded a significant portion of their expedition. When Michiri caught wind of this, she contacted each of Moni's sponsors and tried to convince them to withdraw their support for Moni and sponsor her instead. Her subversion was partly successful and cost the Rotary team a substantial amount of sponsorship money, money that could have bought seventeen bottles of oxygen or supplied food for the expedition.

Sensing his daughter's frustration, Mohan encouraged Moni to focus on the goal. Although he didn't know much about Moni's relationship with Michiri, Mohan knew Michiri's family and speculated about the reasons for her animosity. Years earlier, when Michiri's father died, three contiguous parcels of family land went up for sale by lottery. Mohan purchased the lot adjacent to the road and built a sixteen-room tourism guest house that shared a courtyard with the interior lots owned and occupied by Michiri's brothers. Based on their interactions over the years, Mohan surmised that Michiri's bitterness had something to do with the land transaction.

"I had the sense that the family was angry that an outsider bought into the family land," Mohan said.

Things were not going well for Michiri, though. Desperate, unable to raise more funding and find her own experienced expedition team, she called a private meeting with the Nepal Rotarian committee and proposed to join Moni's team. The Rotarian committee called Moni to a meeting and asked if she would invite Michiri to join the Rotary Nepal Centennial Everest Expedition team. After consulting with her team, they were all in agreement that adding Michiri would be too dangerous. Choosing an experienced team that you trust deeply is a key factor in a safe and successful summit bid. With their knowledge and experience summiting Everest, Pem and Kami were well-aware of how expeditions can be hindered by horrific weather, consequential accidents, and the stress of higher altitudes at Camps III and IV, and the sixteen-hour summit push at night, followed by the treacherous descent. They also knew that disorganization, chaos, and infighting within a team would doom their expedition from the start. Moni, Pem, and Kami trusted each other explicitly, and there was no mistaking the fact that adding Michiri would cause unwanted trouble for the expedition. When Moni shared the team's decision and rationale with the Rotarian committee, they concurred and kept the original three team members. Michiri would have to continue looking for a team or climb on her own with a guide.

LUKLA TO EVEREST BASECAMP

Expedition Day 1
9,383ft - 17,598ft

To reach Everest Basecamp from Lukla, the team trekked for eight days through the bucolic Khumbu region villages of Phadking, Monzo, Namche Bazaar, Tengboche, and Dingboche, staying at teahouses along the way, traveling the same route as Tenzing Norgay and Edmund Hillary.

They stopped in Namche, 11,286 feet to acclimatize. While there, they rested, called family, hiked, and visited the Sherpa Culture Museum, where the team explored the artifacts and talked with local photographer and museum owner, Lhakpa Sonam. At the museum exit, they looked through the Sherpa photograph gallery, stopping at the first photo, the famous 1953 photo of Tenzing Norgay and Sir Edmund Hillary. Moni moved down the chronological photos and found Kami's photo, but Pem's 2004 summit picture and bio were missing. At the very end of the exhibit, she grew excited.

"When I saw ten pictures of ladies who summited Everest, I hoped my picture would make it there one day, too!" she said.

Pem and Kami came up behind her and joked, *"Maybe you'll be the Newari girl on the wall with Sherpa ladies."*

EVEREST BASECAMP

Expedition Day 8
17,598ft / 5,364m

The Rotary team reached Everest Basecamp on April 5th. For the expedition's duration, this would be home base, a resting place while they acclimated to higher altitudes and waited for a weather window to summit. Everest Basecamp (EBC) sits on the Khumbu glacier, the highest glacier in the world, and is the last habitable place climbers live while preparing for the summit. During climbing seasons, the otherwise raw, gloomy, barren glacier turns into a colorful tent city of bright yellow, orange, red, and blue. The tents pop up early season and migrate steadily downslope as hundreds of climbers, photographers, cooks, dishwashers, porters, guides, and team managers hike up to set up camp. By early April of the spring climbing season, the slope is bursting with rudimentary camp sites and cook tents, reaching a population as high as 1,500.

Climbers can spend weeks and months on Everest, complete their acclimatization rotations and never get a weather window, a period of four or five consecutive days before a summit attempt when the weather-producing jet stream moves north away from the mountain and winds calm to below 40 mph. Winds below 10 mph are advisable for a summit bid. These brief calm periods typically occur in the second or third week of May, just before monsoons gather in the Bay of Bengal and batter the Khumbu Valley with snow and rain.

With the easiest leg of the expedition behind them, Pem, Moni, and Kami made camp. A comfortable stay at EBC hinges on a solid, level campsite. EBC sits on the lower end of the sloping glacier, a half-mile-long river of moving ice. In 1995, scientific studies showed the Khumbu glacier moving at a rate of three to four feet a day. The only way to sleep on a steep incline at 17,598 feet is to find a tent site as flat as possible, make it flatter, and push aside the fear that the earth beneath you is moving and might crack open and swallow you. Securing a tent against wind and potential avalanche in ice, rock, and gravel on a steep, moving glacier is no easy task. The Rotary team set their packs on the icy ground and fanned out in search of the flattest available site and spent the afternoon dragging flat rocks over to level the campsite.

Not long after the team arrived at EBC, Pemba dai, the team's hired cook, arrived to assemble the expedition cook tent, dining area, and his personal sleeping quarters. Pemba dai, as Moni respectfully calls him, a distant cousin of Pem's, left Chyangba Village when he was a teen to find work in Kathmandu. He was a decent cook and a good fit for the job with a mix of experience in remote, high elevation cooking. He had worked for Wongchu's company, Peak Promotion, as well as local Himalaya trekking companies that offered guided camping trips at lower elevations.

Pemba was a brawny 5'7," and had jowly, dimpled cheeks. His smile was wide and slightly lopsided with a hint of mischief. He was easygoing and always prepared meals on time, Pem said, unlike many EBC cooks he knew. Plus, he cooked whatever the team asked for. Moni loved Pemba's dal bhat and said that his double-boiler cake was to die for.

Back at home in Kathmandu, Pemba had a wife and three children, a girl and two boys.

He was a quiet man. After cleaning up, most expedition cooks roamed from tent to tent playing cards and socializing, some quite boisterously if alcohol was consumed. But fraternizing was not Pemba's thing. When his daily work was done, Pemba went directly to his tent to sleep.

The Basecamp kitchen is a critical infrastructure for every climbing expedition. Each expedition team sets up their own (or shared) cook camp with a cook, a cook tent, and a separate dining tent. Higher above Basecamp, most climbers, unless they've hired a porter, pack and prepare their own camp-style meals on a small propane stove, eating dehydrated meals, noodles, broth, oatmeal, and dried foods. It's too difficult to get fresh meat, vegetables, and fruit beyond EBC, and besides, at that altitude, climbers have no appetite and resort to forcing themselves to eat the simplest of proteins like nuts, chocolate, and dried beef sticks. Large expedition teams often employ a head cook and a second cook, especially if they set up for meals at Camps I and II. The second cook is usually assigned to work at the higher camps.

Cooking at EBC is a tricky enterprise and a lot goes into keeping a good kitchen. All food is carried up on the backs of mules, yaks, and Sherpas. The transportation from Lukla takes days, and the lack of refrigeration creates a food safety concern. To avoid food poisoning, climbers must be careful about what they eat, especially meats, and a vegetarian diet is recommended. Hygiene is critical to the health of the climbers, as well as balanced meals for sustaining energy for weeks and months at high altitude. In addition to preparing healthy food on the expedition team's climbing schedule, a lot of a cook's time and energy is spent collecting, lugging, purifying, and boiling water for two to three months of cooking, cleaning, and bathing. A single shower takes an entire bucket of water.

Sherpas typically eat either in the cook's tent or a separate Sherpa tent away from the climbers' dining tent. According to Pem, one reason behind separate cooking and dining spaces has to do with shielding paying climbers from the questionable hygiene practices of food preparation and storage. Sometimes, meats have spoiled by the time they reach Basecamp after being carried up the mountain unrefrigerated, exposed and surrounded by flies. Dirty eggs are stowed in flour sacks to prevent breakage, and tortillas are made from potentially contaminated flour. Conserving water and fuel used in the gas cook stoves is paramount at elevation, and that necessity, combined with the lack of hot, running water, makes the cleaning of pots and cooking utensils a dubious process, often not up to proper health standards. No one wants to see this.

With camp set up, they began the acclimatization process, which takes several weeks, and considerably longer if complicated by illness or bad weather. To prepare for the summit, the Rotary team planned to spend their first couple of weeks on rotation climbs up to higher camps, returning to

Basecamp for several days of rest, slowly increasing elevation to allow their bodies to adjust and receive more oxygen to muscles and tissues. For first-time Everest climbers, it's important to become familiar with the summit route in case something goes wrong. Teammates, experienced leaders, and even seasoned guides can get in trouble high up on the mountain, leaving climbers on their own. Depending on weather and health, an approximate three-week acclimatizing and summit bid schedule might look like this:

Week 1: EBC to the Khumbu Icefall for a reconnaissance day.

EBC through the Khumbu Icefall and up to Camp I. Spend one or two nights at C1.

Move to Camp II and spend one night at C2.

Descend to EBC. Rest one to three days.

Week 2: EBC directly to Camp II. Rest Day at C2.

Ascend to Camp III, stay a few hours, then descend back to C2.

Spend one to two nights at C2. Descend to EBC for rest day(s).

After acclimatizing, climbers wait for a weather window. If poor weather conditions persist, as is frequently the case at Everest, some climbers drop back down to Dingboche or Pangboche to relax at lower elevations while constantly tuned into meteorological forecasts and reports from EBC.

Acclimatized, fit climbers who retain their health and experience no unmerciful calamities, can reach the summit given a four to five-day fair-weather window. A summit day climbing schedule moves quickly to take advantage of the good weather and get off the mountain quickly for self-preservation.

Week 3: Summit Bid

Day 1: EBC directly to Camp II.

Day 2: Rest day at C2.

Day 3: Camp II to Camp III.

Day 4: Camp III to Camp IV (South Col), the base for summit bid. Rest a few hours.

Day 4/5: 10 p.m. depart Camp IV (South Col) and climb to summit in darkness.

Day 5: Early a.m. summit with 15 to 20 minutes at the top, then descend to C4 (South Col). Rest at the South Col before descent to C2.

Day 6: Camp II to EBC if able to make an early transit through the Khumbu Icefall.

Or descend to Camp I or II and overnight. Then descend to EBC the following day with an early morning descent through the Khumbu Icefall.

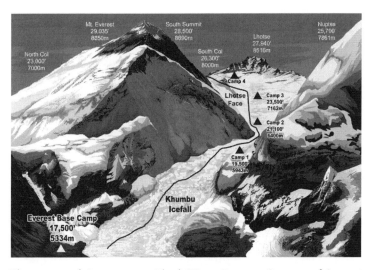

Elevations and Approximate Climb Times Between Camps and Summit
Courtesy of www.alanarnette.com © reproduction prohibited
without authorization

- Everest Basecamp: 17,500'/ 5334m
- C1: 3-6 hours, 1.62 miles
- C2: 2-3 hours, 1.74 miles
- C3: 3-7 hours, 1.64 miles
- Yellow Band: 1-3 hours
- Geneva Spur: 1-2 hours
- C4 / South Col: 1 hour Death Zone
- Balcony: 3-6 hours (the only place for climbers to rest on summit route)
- South Summit: 3-5 hours

- Hillary Step: 30 minutes to 1 hour (the 200-foot final climb over a rock face was erased by the 2015 earthquake. Climb made on fixed ropes, one climber ascending or descending at a time)
- Summit: 1 hour
- Return to C4 / South Col: 3-7 hours
- Return to C2: 3 hours
- Return to Everest Basecamp: 4 hours

Acclimatization requires frequent climbs on ropes and ladders through the Khumbu Icefall, sometimes in the afternoon, when it is most dangerous. Climbers who already know the route to Camp III often skip acclimatization there because sleep deprivation at that altitude wears down the body. With each climb up and back the same day, or overnight at high altitude, climbers lose strength and stamina, especially at Camps III and IV, where the pitch is steep and icy and the air is so thin.

The team's first week at Basecamp was riddled with altitude issues. None of them slept well. On the glacier, the constant creak and groan of rock and ice separating and the loud rumble of avalanches and falling rock kept them awake.

"The sounds were really scary," Pem said. The ground moved as they slept. Each morning, they inspected their tent site to see if it required re-leveling. "Sometimes we would wake up in the morning in a different position than when we went to bed," Pem said.

One night, they heard a close, loud crack. The glacier tore open near their tent, forcing them to relocate their entire camp.

Pem and Moni both suffered from high altitude headaches. Pem decided to ride out the discomfort without medication or descent. Moni picked up a prescription for Diamox from the Basecamp doctor. She had already also lost her appetite, a common problem at higher altitudes, and a challenge to maintain strength. Kami felt fair enough, except for sleep deprivation.

With little to do all day, Moni was bored—another troublesome symptom of a high-altitude expedition. Days, weeks, and months can pass with little to do except the mundane: melt snow for water, acclimatize, plan and replan for the summit attempt, eat, sleep, play cards, walk around camp, visit with other expedition teams, watch movies, and breathe, breathe. Breathe.

The simple act of breathing at Everest takes an extraordinary amount of energy. The oxygen-deprived body, stressed, overworked, and tired, wants to do nothing but sleep.

"It's strange," Pem said. You want to sleep all the time."

Managing altitude sickness and logistical problems— headaches, digestion problems, weight loss, eye issues, colds, flu, pneumonia, supplies not arriving on time or at all—is enough to drive anyone back down the mountain to Kathmandu and the warm comforts of home.

Once they settled into Basecamp, the team began planning acclimatization rotations up the mountain. Pem and Kami were familiar with the Everest route, the terrain, the demands of higher climbs, and the pacing required to reach each Camp. After assessing their individual and team strengths and weaknesses in that moment, the team decided that Pem and Kami would make any extra climbs to Camps II, III, and IV and carry all gear and oxygen tanks needed to set up advance camps. To maintain energy and strength for the summit bid, the team planned that Moni would limit her acclimatization trips to one night each at Camps I, II and III. However, the best laid plans were not so orderly. Higher altitude overnights were delayed, extended, and even skipped as weather, logistics, and physical and emotional variables forced changes, sometimes requiring an instant decision and deviation in plans.

PUJA, EVEREST BASECAMP

Expedition Day 15
April 11, 2005

It was windy and cold at Basecamp that day, a continuation of the prevailing weather pattern that had held steady the previous week. But today was an auspicious day—a day to celebrate. Several of the expeditions, including the Rotary Nepal Centennial Everest Expedition, hired a *lama*, a Tibetan holy monk, to determine the most auspicious day to begin the Everest climb. The lama blessed Monday, April 11. Energy picked up throughout Basecamp, especially with Sherpa climbers and porters preparing to move supplies and gear up the mountain. Following Tibetan Buddhist tradition, Sherpas believe that the Himalaya mountains are the home of mountain gods who must be appeased before they climb.

The intention of this puja ceremony, Moni explained, "is like asking Everest for special permission to climb. We are stepping on you. Please goddess Everest, keep us safe."

That morning, Pemba dai was at another expedition camp, decorating a cake for the EBC doctor and his bride who were marrying later that day. When he returned, he built a stone altar—a pyramid of mountain stones piled skyward with a space in the center for burning juniper branches and incense—just outside the Rotary tent. Each expedition team builds their own shrine at EBC.

While Pem and Kami were off somewhere, Moni decided to shower. At Basecamp, showering is a bucket of cold water poured over your head and body while standing in open air just below your tent. Moni was pouring cold water over her head when Kami returned. Surprised to see her showering and exposed to the cold, he ran to get more water and poured it over her hair, rinsing quickly.

"Moni, you could get sick in this cold," he admonished in his naturally soft and kind, but concerned voice.

She hurried back to the tent and dressed quickly for the puja.

The team members placed their gear on the altar—ice axes, helmets, harness, and a few personal items along with the Rotary Nepal Centennial Everest Expedition flag. Moni added a few things her mom had given her—a *mala* of prayer beads, and Ganesh. When the lama arrived at their shrine, he read from a *Cho*, a script much like a Bible, according to Pem. A strong juniper scent rose in the air as the lama offered rice and flowers to the gods, praying for a safe passage and forgiveness. Pem, Kami, and Moni threw rice toward Everest and over the shrine where their gear was piled.

When the puja ended, in a haze of juniper smoke, the Rotary team strung colorful prayer flags above the altar, their prayers carried off by the wind. High in the clouds, in the energizing spiritual atmosphere of the puja, their prayer flags fluttered. They stood together in silence listening to the mountain. Unless there was a sign from the gods, or one of them got a bad feeling, they would start the climb tomorrow.

Though in practice, some Sherpas, even if they had a bad feeling, would climb, as they depended on the income.

While watching other pujas from a distance, Moni was astonished by the cultural differences she saw. *Why*, she wondered, *would Sherpas eat first and then sit for a puja, and why were they wearing shoes?*

"In our Newari tradition, we are not allowed to eat until the puja ceremony is over," she said. "And no shoes are allowed, no leather goods."

The team spent the day getting ready for the climb into the Khumbu Icefall and the first ascent to Camp I. A Nepali government-issued entry permit is required to enter the Icefall, the official start of the Everest climb. The next day, Kami and Moni would climb the Icefall and return to Basecamp while Pem descended to Dingboche to meet friends and pick up supplies. When Pem returned, they planned to cross the Icefall again together and ascend to Camp I for their first high camp acclimatization.

The morning of April 12, Moni took her first steps into the Khumbu Icefall with Kami.

"I felt uneasy. My shoes didn't fit, and it felt dangerous to walk in them, but I had no choice," she said.

She had searched everywhere but had been unable to find men's or women's climbing shoes that fit her small feet. To take up the extra room in her boots, she wore three pairs of socks.

Their practice climb in the Icefall was without incident. Kami was adept at climbing the seracs and confident crossing the long ladders laid over the crevasses, but Moni was scared and cautious. She had little experience with crampons and traversed slowly. Kami encouraged her on.

Moni Mulepati and Kami Sherpa in the Khumbu Icefall, 2005
Altitude 18,000 ft / 5486 m

Kami Sherpa crossing several ladders lashed together in the Khumbu Icefall

The following morning, Pem, Moni, and Kami left at 6 a.m. for Camp I to deliver supplies they would use on their summit bid. For a higher probability of safety, climbers often depart between 3 and 5 a.m., well before the sun warms the glacier and destabilizes the Icefall. Since they didn't plan to stay the night at Camp I, they would have to cross the Icefall twice. Late in the day, the Icefall crossing was even more dangerous.

They reached Camp I just after noon.

"God, getting to Camp I was very tough," Moni said. "I felt like crying."

At 19,500 feet, walking in crampons proved tedious for Moni. She was tired and out of breath. Once her socks became soaked with sweat, she had to change each extra layer to avoid frostbite, and with little experience using crampons, she took her time getting accustomed to them.

"There's a big learning curve to using crampons safely," she said. "When I was in the mountaineering course, I had to practice separating my feet, so the crampons didn't grab my pants and trip me."

Walking across the long swaying ladders was a balancing act.

"It's partly walking like a zombie, and partly like gracefully walking in a fashion show," she said.

There are other logistical issues encountered in the Icefall, urgent situations one might not consider until they happened.

"It's a real problem when you suddenly have to go to the bathroom while on a ladder," Moni said. "At first, it's awkward, but you get used to it. You really don't have the energy to think about those embarrassing things at that altitude—you just worry about the basics of getting up and down safely."

Thinking about the environmental and health hazards of thousands of people using the ground as a toilet is low on an Everest climber's worry list.

After climbing for over five hours, the team reached the ladder pinned against the towering ice wall that leads to the Western Cwm just below Camp I. The Western Cwm situated between the Khumbu Icefall and Camp I, is a glaciated valley surrounded by three mountain walls—Mt. Everest, Lhotse, and Nuptse.

Pem, Kami, and Moni stopped to rest and assess their physical and mental endurance. It was at least another hour to climb up to Camp I and Moni was exhausted. Since Pem and Kami had energy in reserve and the weather was decent, the team decided that the two men would continue up to Camp I to deliver supplies and set up camp while Moni climbed back down to EBC with a group of Sherpas. Moni's rest days were filled with chores—boiling water, giving interviews, doing laundry, and hanging out with climbers from other expeditions. She washed her clothes at Basecamp for the first time.

"It was freezing," she said. "The water was warm, but when you hang the clothes out to dry, they stiffen up with ice."

She got a letter and package from home, which raised her spirits. Her mother had sent beaten rice and dried meat, a special treat. Later that day, Pem and Kami returned to Basecamp to rest.

Pem went up to Camp I again a few days later and returned exhausted. Moni gave him a glass of juice to revive him.

"We go to Camp I to sleep tomorrow," he said, but Moni had received word that a group of family friends were trekking to Basecamp to deliver supplies and visit, so they postponed their Camp I acclimatization.

Moni heard her friend Abin's voice outside her tent shouting, "Moni, Moni," as he searched for her. She had been feeling tired and a little low-spirited since her attempt to climb to Camp I. The Icefall traverse and the physical challenge at altitude had unnerved her and left her feeling isolated and riddled with doubt. Though the weather was good for a Camp I acclimatization, Pem thought it might lift Moni's spirit and motivation to enjoy a social visit.

"I was so happy when I heard Abin's voice, I jumped outside my tent," Moni said.

The group walked up to the Icefall together and took photographs. Moni's friends marveled at the enormous seracs staggered up through the glacier below the Lhotse face. Kami gave an interview to Nepal TV, and they all returned to EBC to mingle with other expedition teams. Attempting Everest from the South Col that year, along with others, were Mountain Madness, Alpine Ascents, Seven Summits, Adventure Consultants, Everest Parivar Expeditions, IMG, and an Iranian expedition.

Moni turned around to see that her friends had gone over to Michiri's tent and were sitting outside having tea and talking animatedly. Michiri never joined an expedition team, but rumor had it that she had hired a Sherpa to guide her to the summit. They were all talking animatedly. Moni froze and shook with fury and waited in the distance for her friends to rejoin her. Nerves began to fray as expedition fatigue and competitive provocation set in, resulting in a misuse of energy that could affect the whole team's motivation and achievement.

Pem and Kami stayed with Moni and tried to diffuse the situation until her friends rejoined them. On the walk back to their camp, Moni explained what Michiri had done to undermine her team and described her flirtatious behavior. In the first few days at EBC, there were flirty looks and coy laughs, a teasing touch of an arm or shoulder, but before long, Michiri was sitting boldly in the Sherpas' laps. The men didn't mind. They swarmed around her and flirted back, offering her chocolate, helping her carry her backpack, each vying for her attention and the chance to sit close to her in the dining tent.

Under the Newari social norms Moni grew up with, young women did not flirt with or touch a man they were not married to, or at least spoken for by formal engagement. In Moni's mind, Michiri's flirtations felt aggressive and offensive, and she worried that being around her would harm her own reputation. She kept her distance.

"The men greeted me with a respectful *Namaste*," she said, "but openly hugged Michiri."

According to Moni, if you hung around Basecamp and picked up on the Nepali social cues, it was obvious which women were respected by the way men greeted them. In Newari tradition, that form of respect was critical to family honor and the ability of Newari women to find a suitable marriage partner.

If in fact Michiri's flirtatious behaviors tainted her reputation, it made no difference to the men vying for her attention. Their reputations would remain intact.

"Just forget it," Abin dai said to Moni, offering friendly advice. "Don't keep anything about her inside you because it will decrease your energy. One day you will be good friends."

"Never ever!" Moni wrote in a long page of wrath in the expedition journal she kept.

Michiri rattled Moni. Pages of scorching entries appeared in her journal with each encounter. When Michiri got under Moni's skin, Pem would act as coach and help redirect her thoughts.

"Don't pay attention to her," he'd say. "You are a better climber. Keep energy focused on the climb."

Moni would stew for a while, then refocus.

Her daily entries of their 64-day expedition, all 175 pages written in English, her second language, gives a sense of what day to day life was like in the extreme environment—the mundane, the exciting, the horrors, and hopes, both realized and shattered. Her notes illustrate the binary opposites that can arise in extreme expedition-style climbing, such as how climbers must rely on others and a network of support to be successful *and* have a strong degree of self-sufficiency. They reflect how the mind learns to move from preparation to performance, and what happens to the body and mind over a long stretch of time at high altitude—what the brain can take in and focus on, what distracts, and what remains in the shadowy mist of Everest.

"Pem and Kami dai both encouraged and inspired me constantly. When I was low, even with Michiri, they told me to dig deeper, because I'm representing hope for Nepalis."

A larger personal quest behind the Rotary team's summit attempt was a fight for social justice and to cast light on the role of Sherpas in mountaineering. As Moni became drawn to the idea of climbing Everest, she hoped to break barriers for other Nepali women, no matter what caste they were born into. The potential impact of the team's success weighed heavily on her, especially at extreme altitudes when she desperately wanted to get off the deadly mountain and go home.

For centuries, Nepali women have suffered ghastly, pervasive inequalities. The list is long and to this day remains unchanged in many ways—physical violence, poverty, hard work in agricultural fields, class and gender bias, the dowry system and arranged marriages, child marriage, trafficking. Nepali women are prohibited from inheriting property or owning and controlling land.

In the harsh cultural practice of *chhaupadi*, menstruating women and girls are forbidden to stay in their homes or participate in family events and are sent to live in primitive huts or sheds, often with no heat or plumbing. The cultural belief behind this practice is the notion that menstruating women are considered impure or dirty, and that they will bring bad fortune to their families. Chhaupadi has existed for hundreds of years and despite having been outlawed in Nepal in 2017, is still widely practiced. Many women and girls have died from the cold, woodsmoke, and animal attacks while banished to these crude outbuildings.

Over the history of Everest climbing, more than 300 climbers have died on Everest, their bodies left on the mountain, the majority being Sherpa mountaineers and porters. Despite their significant contributions to Everest mountaineering and making the summit possible for foreigners, very few Sherpa stories have made it into the vast canon of climbing literature. Sherpa lives and deaths and their roles in the business of Everest have remained obscure.

"Sherpas climb all the time," Moni said, "but it doesn't matter unless you do something special, something different from what others have done, like break a record. And that is true," she said wistfully, her face suddenly serious. "We are no one, but we keep climbing. If we succeed, we will be known. I remember this always," she said with a noticeable edge of irritation and pride in her voice, mindful of the disturbing inequity and lack of recognition of Sherpa mountaineers and Nepali women.

Back at Basecamp, Moni's visitors stayed for a meal of chapati and curry. She hoped they would spend the night, but they needed to get back. They left her with the goodies they had ferried up the mountain: two cans of Pringles, Snickers bars, a Toblerone bar, and *kaju* nuts. Before saying goodbyes, she gave Abai dai a list of items the team needed for the expedition and where to find them. As soon as they left, a current of homesickness struck Moni.

"When I saw Mom and Dad's picture in my tent, I started crying and couldn't stop. I cried for two hours."

Worried, Pem went to Moni's tent and tried to calm her down. He encouraged her to focus on a specific goal. Their success and lives depended on the team's full concentration. It's like climbing in self-defense mode.

"You need to be positive and focus on climbing. Tomorrow we climb to Camp I," he said.

There's a certain psychology associated with summiting Everest, and at some point, nerves and irritability set in. No matter how strong-willed and mentally tough one is, a summit bid is ultimately a race against time, money, and weather with a constant threat of danger, injury, psychological breakdown, and death. As the days march on, living in discomfort in a hostile environment that literally sucks the life out of you, where you can't eat or sleep and feel miserable most of the time, the mind warps and tempers wear thin. Anxieties rise, and desires and purpose unravel or become confused, no matter what the reason is for summiting. It's easy to see how an archrival can become a mind trap. High up in thin air, it takes constant renegotiation to ease the mind back to normal boundaries of reality, sometimes requiring the help of a teammate, friend, or guide to help refocus. For Moni, her greatest rival had become a double-edged sword, at times motivating her forward, but also depleting her mental energy.

Pem managed his own stress in a different way, he said, "by never putting too much expectation on things." It was pointless to get frustrated or upset with a change of plans due to weather, sickness, or timing.

"You have to go with nature, you can't control it," he added. "Besides, if not on the mountain, I would be in Kathmandu. Here, I can play cards, they feed you, and the mountain is like home."

Pem speculates that his easy way of being was related to his childhood.

"It's probably because I left home at a young age, and often had no place to sleep. If hungry, there was nothing to eat, no one to make food," he said. He also learned to adjust his expectations. "When you're not powerful enough, people always step on your dreams. If you have an expectation and can't achieve it, you have to let go of expectations," he said.

Pem also knew, as did Kami, that not everyone would make it.

As Kami pointed out, "Even if everything goes right—planning, timing, the weather—sometimes the body doesn't favor getting to the summit."

CAMP I ACCLIMATIZATION

Expedition Day 25
April 25, 2005

By 4:30 a.m., Pem and Moni were packed and headed for Camp I. They were deep in the Khumbu Icefall, climbing at a steady pace, when a piercing *crack* ricocheted through the ice like a gunshot. Pem, just ahead of Moni, turned toward the sound. Moni stopped dead in her tracks and watched the entire platform of ice beneath her feet disappear with a *whoosh, thoonk.*

"It felt like an earthquake," she said. "I stepped backwards to safety, but my legs were shaking."

Physically unharmed, but rattled, she continued following Pem across a set of eight ladders joined together by rope. Pem was already on solid ground above the ladder when suddenly, another sharp *crack*, like a clap of thunder, blasted through the air. Moni looked up to see a massive chunk of ice hurtling down toward her. It happened so fast that there wasn't much to do but clench the safety rope and lean to the side as much as possible without falling. A huge, gray wall of ice whizzed by inches from the ladder and disappeared into the crevasse.

"I heard a *crack* then *bloong*. It sounded like a bomb, like we were in a war zone. Always look up when you hear that *clink* or *crack* sound," she said. "An avalanche might be coming."

At the sound of the first *boom*, the string of climbers ahead of Pem scrambled up higher until the sounds stopped and they could relax a bit. Pem had turned back to make sure Moni was okay and coached her forward.

"I got scared and it took me forever to finish crossing that ladder," Moni said.

When she was finally off the ladder, she let Pem know that she was angry with him for walking too far ahead and not watching out for her safety. She felt that he was too far away to offer help if she was in trouble. Many climbers don't survive these incidents and they both knew they got lucky and dodged a bullet. As Moni recounted the story, Pem laughed quietly, lowering his head sheepishly. Moni elbowed him in the ribs and smiled. Soon, they were back in a cautious climbing rhythm, eager to be out of the Icefall.

Ascending the last section of the Icefall up the long ladder that led to the Western Cwm, the glacial valley below Camp I, frightened Moni. Her mood turned gloomy as she looked up at the top of the monstrous ice tower and series of ladders. The Icefall Doctors had strapped the five ladders together and screwed the top and bottom into the ice earlier in the season. Pem and Moni couldn't help but wonder if the ladder was still secure given weathering and shifting ice, and Moni was still jittery from the close call earlier in the Icefall.

On April 21 at 12:45 p.m., they reached Camp I. By the time they got to camp, the weather had changed to snow, and the temperature had dropped. The tent had already been set up by Pem and Kami, so they stuffed their camping pads inside, removed their crampons, and crawled in to get warm.

Three weeks into their expedition, Moni was finally at Camp I, but she had never imagined that Camp I would be so cold and snowy, and the visibility so poor.

"We were surrounded by tall mountains, yet not one peak in sight, nor a person," she said.

Pem put on his down jacket and went back outside, returning with a large clump of snow and ice. He lit the camp stove and melted the ice for drinking water and to cook noodles.

"Why are you doing that?" Moni asked, scrutinizing the snow in the plastic container, her lips pursed, eyebrows drawn down in a disapproving frown.

"Everyone does that here," Pem said. "We have to melt ice if we want to have water to drink."

"But everyone goes to the bathroom here and steps on the ice," Moni protested, her face in a tight grimace.

Pem laughed and assured her that he scooped snow and ice away from the tent where no one had peed or walked, but Moni was not buying it. She had to convince herself and accept that this was mountain life at Everest. Trying to ignore horrible thoughts of drinking filthy, contaminated water, she dug out a can of Pringles from her rucksack, and the small box of mixed dry meat and beaten rice that her mother had sent. She mixed it all up with salami, and while eyeing Pem suspiciously, ate hungrily. Pem opened a can of mango fruit, but it was frozen, so he tossed it in the pan with the ice and made juice. After fueling their bodies, they went to bed. Pem went right to sleep, but Moni was still awake at 2 a.m., tossing and turning in her sleeping bag. It was hot inside the tent and the altitude was affecting her.

As she lay awake, classic imposter syndrome thoughts raced through her mind. She wrote in her journal: "What am I thinking? Why am I doing all this? Can I climb Everest? Complete this mission? What if I can't?" She worried about what people would think of her if she failed and wondered what Pem and Kami really thought of her.

"I knew Moni could do it," Pem said.

Kami wasn't so sure. "She was a very slow climber, and you need to climb faster to reach the summit, especially from Camp IV," he said.

As she laid awake, she reviewed her relationship with Pem. Moni was stubborn and felt irritated with Pem most of the time and frequently argued with him. Pem either ignored her or argued back, depending on the importance of the issue and his energy levels. Kami, she thought, was very strong physically, unlike Pem. Sometimes she thought Pem was selfish.

She looked at the clock every half hour and willed time to pass more quickly. Finally, she fell asleep, but was jolted awake by a bad dream about her father. Moni wanted to call him but had left the satellite phone back in Basecamp. She fell into a restless sleep, but woke up with a pounding headache, as if someone was inside her skull, hammering.

Pem called Kami in Basecamp to get an update, then cooked rara soup. Kami was on his way up to Camp I. Pem handed a cup to Moni and urged her to sip. As he left for Camp II, he gave her a dose of Diamox. They both had planned to ascend to Camp II for Moni's first round of acclimatization there, but with her battering headache and the onset of a menstrual cycle, she had little energy for the climb. Earlier in the season, while on a training climb at Ella Peak with Pem and Kami, she recalled his kindness when, mid-climb, she started her menstrual cycle and lost energy. Pem reached into her pack, removed half her load, and carried it up the mountain for her. It was a gesture of kindness that made her appreciate and trust Pem on big climbs.

For today, the team agreed that Moni would stay behind at Camp I while Pem and Kami climbed to C2. An hour or so after Pem left, Kami arrived at Camp I and rested briefly before heading for Camp II where he and Pem would spend the night. Moni cleaned the tent and slept another night at Camp I. The next day, Pem descended back to Camp I. It was decided that Moni would go back down to Basecamp and rest until she felt stronger. Pem would overnight at Camp I while Kami acclimatized at Camp II one more night.

Moni felt hungry and tired, but ate some chocolate, put on her shoes, and packed her sleeping bag. The altitude caused her to move slowly.

"I was so tired my legs didn't want to move," she said.

Near the long ladder down into the Icefall, she ran into a Sherpa friend who offered to carry her pack and cross the Icefall with her. About 4 p.m. as they reached EBC, a strong snowstorm blew in and covered the tents.

Everyone uses their own mental strategies to cope with the extended time at altitude and the demons that appear, the unexpected situations. While the teammates' personalities were completely opposite—Moni the extroverted, energetic partner, and Pem and Kami more reserved and methodical—they each possessed that 'fire in their belly' that high performers demonstrate, the deep, intrinsic motivation, confidence, self-discipline, and ability to manage stress. At Everest, they also needed to be humble, aware, resilient, fighters.

What kept Pem going was his desire to support his family in Chyangba and a wild, crazy dream to someday immigrate to France or America, and his growing love for Moni.

Moni was inspired to climb Everest to do something for her country, to help put the Nepal Rotary on the world map, to develop tourism, and to promote world peace and understanding—all the things she would say in a formal speech if she summited. But she had personal goals, too. She was motivated to summit by the many family members, Rotarians, and friends who supported her and cheered her on, as well as the potential impact of her success on young Nepali women if she summited—a model for Nepali women to break tradition, and gain status and freedom of expression.

"For me, doing something new that nobody had done before, and showing that women can do the same thing as men, was my main goal," Moni explained. "In Nepal, women are always discouraged. Nepali women who work are not considered good women. They are considered 'fast' and go with a lot of men," she said. "It's hard for Nepali women to marry if they go out a lot or are very social, or if they are not obedient and traditional. They cook, get married, and raise babies. Traditionally women don't work outdoors or outside the home."

Moni was determined to break these rules and traditions and show that women could excel even in traditionally male roles, if given the opportunity.

"I want equal rights and equal freedom," she said.

And she wanted to be loved for being a very intelligent, capable woman.

*   *   *

Back at Basecamp, while the team waited for the weather to clear, they joined an organized group of climbers collecting garbage in the Icefall. Someone found helicopter parts from a crash in 1980. A yak had died on the mountain, requiring human muscle to move it. Pem and a few other climbers went out in the storm to dispose of the carcass.

Once the storm passed, the team continued their rotation schedule. On April 25th, Pem and Kami left EBC at 5 a.m. and climbed to Camp II and back to EBC the same day. Moni stayed at Basecamp to receive food supplies, oxygen tanks, and regulators sent from Kathmandu. They were still short three oxygen tanks needed for the summit bid. Moni called Kathmandu to order more while Pem and Kami tested the oxygen regulators.

The team packed food, oxygen, and clothing in preparation for the team climb to Camp II. Moni was anxious about climbing through the Icefall again and relieved the tension by stitching Rotary badges on each of their packs.

Expedition Day 31
April 27, 2005

Morning came fast. At 4 a.m. the team was up and devouring a batch of pancakes. At 5 a.m., they all walked to the Icefall to begin their climb to Camp II. The weather that day alternated between sun and snow, hot and cold. The Icefall was groaning and cracking all day, but they made it through without incident, arriving at Camp I by noon, giving them plenty of time to rest before the climb to Camp II. Pem and Kami had already set up Camp II, which gave them more time and energy for the climb.

Although the climb from Camp I to II is less than two miles, with an elevation gain of about 1500 feet, it is a hard climb. The Western Cwm is a U-shaped valley carved out by the Khumbu Glacier that funnels down from the Lhotse face. At 22,000 feet, this area holds a different type of danger than the Khumbu Icefall. The valley is steep, filled with enormous crevasses, and can be extremely hot, often reaching a brutal 100 degrees Fahrenheit. The intense sun reflecting off the snow can cause snow blindness even on a cloudy day. On the opposite extreme, a snow or windstorm can make the Western Cwm a dangerously cold climb. Unfortunately for climbers, the steepest section arrives in the last thirty minutes of the climb, when legs and lungs are spent.

Midway up the Western Cwm, Pem caught the first glimpse of Everest and felt a pang of reverence. It's a spiritual feeling to see the mountain, he said.

"Everest is a god for all people in the region. So many villagers' lives have been changed by Everest."

Personally, Pem feels he'd be nowhere without Everest. He would likely be working the fields in Chyangba village.

"Moni, look up," he said, pointing toward the massive peak.

An excitement she hadn't felt for a long time reignited, and she felt a chill.

"For the first time, I have hope we can summit," she told Pem, catching her breath.

As thousands of climbers can attest, the awe of seeing Everest, with its mix of fear and wonder, can do strange things – put you in an altered state of consciousness, inspire a crazed urge to stand on the top of the forbidding peak. Awe has complex physiological and psychological effects that spark changes in the nervous system, producing a sense of diminished self, and challenging one's understanding of the world. Everest's magnetic qualities are undeniable when deep in its presence.

Surprisingly, from the Nepal side, the first view of Mt Everest isn't until part way up the Western Cwm. Although Everest is the highest mountain in the Himalayas, it is invisible from EBC except for one location—a hike up Kala Patthar just west of Gorak Shep. Oddly, even from that vantage point, Everest does not look like the tallest mountain. In an optical illusion, the closer peaks seem higher.

The Rotary team arrived at Camp II at 4 p.m. after a twelve-hour climb. Once settled into their tent, they talked and planned the next rotation while Kami cooked mushroom soup and Pem cut onions and garlic for the dry meat. Dinner was soup and red beaten rice and salami, a welcome treat at high camp, thanks to Shanti, Moni's mother. After dinner, Moni called Kathmandu to check on getting more oxygen tanks and batteries while Pem and Kami packed for their climb to Camp III the next morning.

Spent from the day's climb, they fell into their sleeping bags in the shared tent at 6:30 p.m. Rest was fitful. Headaches plagued all three climbers through the night. Despite feeling altitude sickness, at 5:30 a.m. on April 28th, Pem and Kami departed for Camp III. Pem only made it halfway to Camp III and decided to turn back. He tied up the team's gear on ropes near the edge of the route to be claimed on the next climb.

"The climb was difficult and tiring," Pem told Moni. "I made it halfway up and couldn't go any further. I tied our gear up. Kami went up to Camp III to drop off oxygen bottles and supplies for our Camp III acclimatization and summit day. He will join us later this afternoon."

Kami is soft-spoken and unassuming—bashful, almost. Despite his small frame, he's a strong climber. He climbs fast and with relative ease without oxygen, moving between camps in an hour whereas other climbers make it in three to eight hours.

"I don't know why I can walk so fast," he said. "Sometimes I run."

Most foreign climbers start oxygen at Camp III and can purchase as many tanks as they need, but Sherpas typically wait until they reach Camp IV in the Death Zone. One reason for this relates to an industry rule. Sherpas hired by guiding companies are allotted just two bottles of oxygen for an entire expedition, including all advance camp setups and all climbs and descents with a client. The rationale behind the industry restriction, according to Pem and Kami, is the high cost of oxygen and the natural ability of high-altitude Sherpas to adapt to low-oxygen environments. Yet while Sherpas do have genetically superior anaerobic metabolism compared to Westerners, which allows their blood cells to convert energy into oxygen more efficiently, this is no guarantee that a Sherpa won't get into trouble and need more than two bottles of oxygen. Like all other climbers, Sherpas are not invincible.

On a 2003 expedition climb, Kami recalls running out of oxygen on the South Summit at 28,704 feet. The dome-shaped ice, snow, and limestone peak just below Everest's primary summit is a common place for climbers to change oxygen bottles before the summit push or make the decision to turn around. Kami gulped a last, startling breath before his oxygen quit.

"I felt like a fish out of water," he recalled. "I took a step and couldn't move. My mind was blank, and my body was aching on the *inside*. It was very scary because I still had to go down and couldn't have another oxygen bottle."

Because clients always receive oxygen before the Sherpa support team, a problem arises when clients take so long to climb that porters and guides run out of their limited supply, he explained. It's also not uncommon to have a regulator valve freeze, further limiting the oxygen supply. Pressure builds up and blows out the valve, releasing the remaining oxygen from the tank into the air.

* * *

While Pem rested, Moni boiled water and made soup, and called Basecamp to check for messages. Good news: Wongchu Sherpa at Peak Promotion had their oxygen tanks for the summit bid and was sending them up the mountain. Other news: Michiri might not get a summit permit. Moni took a small amount of pleasure in that possibility.

Kami had successfully dropped off a tent, oxygen tanks, and supplies at Camp III, and was back at Camp II by early evening. The team rummaged through their sparse provisions, looking for dinner inspiration. None of them were hungry, but they had to eat. They settled on soup and noodles, the go-to meal for high-altitude nourishment when hunger fades. It was

Pem's twenty-third birthday that day. Moni treated him to chocolate and wished him a happy birthday in the middle of the night while she lay awake.

Moni woke up sick with a fever and unbearable headache that left her bedridden at 21,300 feet. The best remedy for altitude sickness is to descend to lower elevation as quickly as possible, but that morning, as it commonly does on Everest, foul weather moved in at the most inopportune time. Given the situation, the team decided that Kami would return to Basecamp and bring food back up to Camp II where Moni and Pem would stay and rest. Moni was so incapacitated by the headache she wasn't sure she could move even if her life depended on it.

Kami made good time in the storm, reaching Basecamp in a couple of hours. While waiting for Kami's return, Pem attempted to reconfigure their tent site to reduce the pitch, hoping it would bring them all a better night's sleep.

"The slope was so steep at Camp II, we slid down to the bottom of our tent," Pem said.

He was inside making soup when the Basecamp doctor stopped by to deliver Japanese rice and medication for Moni. When she woke up at 5:30 p.m., she was shocked and relieved to feel clear-headed and hungry.

"What would you like to eat?" Pem asked, a big smile on his face.

"I thought I was dreaming!" Moni said. "I want *pani*, *puri*, pork *ko*, pizza, chow mein, fried rice, sizzler!" she cried out.

Pem laughed. "What do you want to eat *here* at Camp II? This is *not* Kathmandu."

He cooked *rara* noodles with tuna—rice, noodles, and potatoes, in one pot. Moni was already tired of this food and couldn't wait for a real meal. A friend concerned about her health stopped by their tent to check in on Moni and brought fried potatoes.

"Wow! Tasty," Moni howled, her taste buds delighted.

By morning, the weather had improved. Pem and Moni got up at 5 a.m. and planned to move to Camp III. They couldn't stay at altitude much longer and wanted to press on and finish acclimatizing so they could return to Basecamp and rest for a summit bid. Moni felt weak. She brushed her teeth for the first time in three days and vomited. Her tongue burned.

"Why did you brush?" Pem scolded.

After a mug of hot water and another dose of Diamox, Moni felt slightly better, but was still shivering despite the layers of warm clothing she wore—a heavy coat, fleece gloves, and three pairs of socks. She could hardly move and had trouble zipping her coat. Pem reached over and put his hand gently on her forehead, checking for fever, and helped her with her zipper. He dug around in her pack and moved the heavier items into his backpack. By 6:30 a.m. they were walking toward Camp III at a very slow pace.

"You have to move faster," Pem told Moni.

Ahead was the Western Cwm climb followed by Lhotse's relentless ice wall below Camp III. Although the Western Cwm's glacial valley is broad and flat, with an average temperature of about 50 degrees Fahrenheit, the temperatures there can be extreme. On a hot, windless day, it's brutally hot, often 90 degrees.

The Lhotse Face is a tough, vertical climb on hard ice. To reach Camp II, it takes five to ten hours to ascend 2,000 vertical feet at a 40-degree pitch. In comparison, the same vertical climb would take approximately an hour at sea level.

"You have to get into a rhythm of 'kick and pull' all the way up," Pem said.

Climbers kick into the hard, blue glacial ice to establish a crampon hold, then pull on the ropes and step up, using handheld jumars. Jumars are attached to the fixed rope and to a climber's harness and slide up the rope above the climber. Teeth pinch the rope and clamp down, allowing climbers to pull themselves up without slipping down. Each time the jumar is pushed up the rope, the climber ascends a little higher. Rocks regularly fall down the steep face putting climbers in harm's way. As a safety backup, climbers tie into the end of the rope to arrest a fall.

"About every 50 to 100 feet, there's an anchor point screwed into the ice and climbers have to reset their jumar," Pem explained. "On a cold day, lots of climbers get frostbite when they take the jumar out and reset it. Beyond Camp IV, it's difficult and very scary to change the jumar," he said.

Closer to the summit, especially near Camp IV, the Yellowband, and the Hillary Step, there's often a long line of slow climbers and no place to pass except while on fixed ropes.

"To pass another climber is very risky," Pem said. "You have to unclip all your safety lines to go around someone. In places like the Hillary Step, there might be nine different ropes, old and new. You grab them all, hoping you have the right line and it doesn't pull out of the ice."

It's so steep near the top that if a climber slips or falls, they will slide on snow and rocks all the way down to Camp II, Pem said. Once, near the ridge, he recalls passing two climbers sitting on the edge of the route unclipped from the safety ropes and without oxygen.

"It was extremely dangerous."

Challenges for the Rotary team were stacking up: the physical challenge of climbing the Lhotse face plus Everest's fickle weather, the likelihood of worsening altitude sickness, and a seasonal time clock that was running out. They could not hold in place at Camp II much longer because the altitude would deplete them, and it would take a lot out of them physically if they had to descend to Basecamp, only to climb to Camp III again before a summit bid. Each time they climbed, their bodies weakened and required a four-to-five-day rest at Basecamp.

As they neared Camp III, Moni was completely spent. "I can't move up or down," she told Pem.

They stopped for a snack and rested briefly. Pem glanced at his watch.

"We have to go down to Camp II or Basecamp," Pem said as he repacked his rucksack, noticing the bad weather clouds gathering in the sky. "Start walking down. I'll catch up with you."

"Each slow step was hard," Moni recalled.

To force herself to focus and take another step, she talked to God, her mother and father, and spoke everyone's name that she could think of.

About twenty-five minutes later, Pem caught up with her. Getting back to Basecamp meant a dangerously late crossing in the Khumbu Icefall. At the Icefall, they noticed that the entire route had changed since they last climbed. There were more large crevasses. Getting through would require a bit of luck as well as skill, but they pushed on, arriving at Basecamp at 4 p.m. in a whirling snowstorm. From the Icefall, Pem had called ahead and ordered food, which was ready when they arrived.

Moni had developed a concerning eye problem on the way to Camp III, possibly a blood clot from the altitude. Mentally and physically depleted, she considered taking a rescue helicopter to Kathmandu to rest for a few days, but if she made that choice, she might not return. Her journal entries reflected a weary state of mind and a fear that she was in over her head:

> "I feel like going to KTM for a few days. If there's a rescue helicopter I would like to go along for 2-3 days then back. Missing EVERYONE!! HOME, MOM, DAD, SONI, MONISH, FUCHI!!
>
> If I can go to KTM, I can get my eye checked too. Dr. Ian said it's a blood clot due to lack of oxygen. If it grows bigger then I have to stop going up. Worried if I go higher, I might go blind!!
>
> I'll climb Everest only once. If I succeed this time, that is more than enough for me! God climbing Everest is not a JOKE. FULL OF RISK. I'll never suggest anyone to climb Everest. I didn't find as much difficulty climbing Yala and Island Peak. But this is EVEREST! I don't understand why people climb Everest more than 1 time. Maybe Sherpas have to climb for the money. Even they find it really hard."

Recognizing Moni's self-doubt, and concerned that she might give up, Pem and Kami cheered her on, cooked for her, and encouraged her forward.

"Everyone is bound to have a bad day," Kami coached.

Once Moni had rested at lower altitude, showered, and regained her appetite, she revived, although she was still concerned about the possibility that her eye condition could worsen in the Death Zone and leave her blind.

LINGERING SPIRITS

Expedition Day 35
May 1, 2005

The fall came fast, mid-step, tense and wet. Death rose above the gods, above the uppermost air, and funneled down Sargarmatha through the scattered clouds and gorges, bearing down on camps with their frozen orange tents and restless climbers, word spreading furiously down to the villages and fields and tiny houses ringed in wood smoke where families dug potatoes, stacked grass, washed, and hung clothes to dry while desperately listening for word—even the softest whisper—of loved ones. *Was it our loved one?*

Death grants no reprieve on Everest. It comes deep in a crevasse, in the unpredictable ice seracs of the Khumbu Icefall, through the Death Zone high in the troposphere—in the ecosystem where all weather on earth occurs, where planes fly and human bodies wither every second, every step. Death goes down on the squally single track up the mountain, on the Yellowband rock of the Lhotse face, on the Balcony—the last flat spot to rest before the final summit push. Death comes on descent when the body is diminished—a shadow of itself;

when exhaustion has set in and motivation has dwindled after standing on the top of the world.

*   *   *

The handheld radio buzzed and rasped, then went silent. Then came the transmission, crisp and clear: "*A foreign climber has fallen into a crevasse. Rescue assistance needed at the following coordinates.*" Kami and other Sherpas in the vicinity—about twelve in all—dropped what they were doing and converged at the crevasse where the climber had fallen. Standing at the precipice, hands on hips, extra ropes, crampons, and carabiners shifting between their palms, they peered down at the man lying on a narrow ice shelf about 40 feet down.

Rescues are daunting at Everest, sometimes impossible. There are no quick rescues, no helicopters to swoop in at this altitude where the air is too thin to generate enough lift to stay airborne, where the wind and weather are consistently gnarly, and places to land either nonexistent or too dangerous. In the hour it took the Sherpas to climb to the crevasse, the man had quietly passed into death, perfectly alone under the blotchy grey Everest sky.

The dead climber, dressed in a marine yellow jacket and black wind pants, lay supine on a small, icy overhang. He was lying face up, arms tucked almost naturally by his side, a massive snow boulder rising out of the snow beside his head. A pale, gloveless hand protruded from his jacket sleeve, one knee crossed slightly over the other. A set of footprints encircled his body. The climber's guide, the first to the scene, had belayed down to check his client's pulse. Finding none, he carefully pulled the hood over the climber's head and covered his face with a *khada* scarf.

The climber had made it to the summit, bowed in gratitude to his guide, and called his girlfriend and then his father with the exhilarating news. Then, with a surge of glory and the violent Everest wind at his back, he began the long, exhausting, and dangerous descent down to Basecamp. Then he fell. No one saw him. By then, he had been climbing for at least eleven hours straight, most of it in the dark. Speculation was that the climber had unclipped from the fixed safety rope and taken a misstep when his crampon snagged the edge of his pants, sending him stumbling into the crevasse. Somehow, he had become separated from his Sherpa guide and was descending about twenty minutes ahead, too far away for assistance or guidance. Had his fall not been interrupted by a scant ice shelf, the question of what had befallen him would have been of little consequence; his death another statistic, one more mystery in the stone yard of Everest.

Resting on the narrow mantle of ice, the fallen climber looked strangely at peace, as if in repose in a beautiful, snowy coffin. In a wholly different context, minus the 40-foot drop, one could imagine that the climber was dozing in the sunshine, sheltering out of the raw Everest wind, a yellow hat shading his face, taking a rest from high altitude fatigue and a month or two of living on Everest.

At the brink of the crevasse, the Sherpas circled up, talking spiritedly as they assessed the situation and developed a plan for what had become a body extrication. They evaluated ice conditions, where to secure anchors, the angle of approach, and the gear each Sherpa had on their body or tucked in their backpacks for rigging a sled and lift. One Sherpa took the lead, assigned roles, and delivered instructions like a job foreman, while the others nodded, dispersed, and got to work on rigging a pulley system. Five Sherpas clipped into a fixed rope and rappelled down the ice wall and stood next to the corpse. In the cramped margin of snow around the body, there was just enough room for them to maneuver as long as no one overstepped to the side or backward. Once the sled lowered, they wrapped the body in a blue blanket and lashed it to a flimsy, bright orange sled. Above, the other Sherpas formed a human chain on the upslope, digging their crampons and ice axes into the snow. Eyes cast down, they shouted in chorus—*tan nu, tan nu*—hoisting the sled conveying the dead man in a slow, controlled lift. From the ledge below, two Sherpas climbed up the ice wall to steady and disentangle the sled as it serpentined upward, twisting in one direction and then the other as it rose. Halfway to the top, the corpse careened out of control, snagged, and halted on a lip of ice. From above, the leader shouted orders down into the crevasse. His breathing strained, chest heaving from pulling the unyielding sled, he suddenly bellowed in English, *"Fucking!"*

Pulling halted. Ropes slackened and the corpse accelerated into a free fall. The Sherpas uphill toppled over in the snow. Someone laughed and the laughter swept nervously up the line. The outburst might have been a crass response and lack of sensitivity, Pem explained, having seen occasions when Sherpas cheered when retrieving a body. But he thought it more likely that in the moment, these climbers had become desensitized—the dead bodies spread across Everest no longer a shock. The collective response could have been attributed to a loss of normal social embarrassment that takes place at Everest—like going to the bathroom in privacy, or as simple as the obvious fact that *on Everest, it is fucking hard to pull a dead body up a crevasse and down the mountain, and this could be one of us.* Every Sherpa standing near the corpse knew that the same peril of disappearing into a crevasse, dying from lack of oxygen, hypothermia, being caught in a storm or avalanche or hit by an errant falling boulder, or assisting a client in trouble, could happen to them, too, with the same harsh, irreparable blow to their loved ones.

This climber had, in essence, paid a lot of money to die there on the frozen slopes and crevasses of Mount Everest in a passionate gamble for a remote chance to master something as perilous as summiting a 29,000-foot mountain. In current times, it is commonly known that climbers share an "every climber for themselves" attitude, where dead bodies are left where they fall, climbed over on the cold, remote mountain, barely given a thought. Sometimes, if a dead body is too visible and deemed a hinderance to tourism, it is nudged into a crevasse.

Finally, after much coaxing, the sled freed itself and the Sherpas hoisted it to the top. They grew quiet as the corpse crested the rim and landed with a soft scrape and *whump*. They lingered, studying the body as they fiddled with their gear, acknowledging each other for getting the job done with handshakes and *namastes*, releasing their ties to this specific body with a guarded *nying je*—a generosity of spirit and warm-heartedness.

This was not the first corpse Pem or Kami had seen on Everest. The previous year, from a distance, Pem had observed dead bodies scattered all along the route. Perfectly preserved bodies that had been hemmed in snow and ice for years, like "Green Boots," one of eight climbers who died in the disastrous storm of 1996 chronicled in Jon Krakauer's book, *Into Thin Air*, and the movie *Everest*. The climber's corpse, frozen in near fetal position, cocooned in bright green boots, purple down pants, and a blazing orange jacket, had become a guidepost to the summit, his Day-Glo green boots tagging the 26,000' elevation mark, the entrance to the Death Zone.

"The more bodies you see, the more normal it feels," Pem admitted. But what he felt in the presence of this corpse was different—more disquieting and touching in an emotionally tragic way. "This was not like Green Boots, a climber who had been dead a long time; this was a *fresh* dead body," he said.

When Pem first heard the call on the satellite radio, he expected to rescue a climber in trouble, not to be in the presence of someone so close to their last breath.

When a body is retrieved at Everest, it's not as if you can deliver it to a funeral parlor in a matter of a few hours and be done with it. Bodies are carried down the mountain slowly, awkwardly, dangerously, one camp at a time, and must be carried close to the person transporting it, for safety. In higher Camps, a corpse is clipped to the front of a tent to avoid the risk of body and sled sliding away into the abyss—lost forever in the wild shadows of Everest.

Since the rescue mission had turned into a body retrieval, each Sherpa would get paid $100 for taking the body down to Basecamp and across the dangerous ladders in the Khumbu Icefall. From Basecamp, the deceased climber would be helicoptered to Kathmandu and retrieved by his family.

The guide notified the father of his son's death, his awkward words attempting to speak the unspeakable. The father's shock was deep and silent. He was unprepared. It made no sense. Just an hour ago, he had heard his son's weary but elated voice. As soon as the guide ended the call, he and five other Sherpas began carrying the body down to Basecamp.

The next morning, the Rotary team woke to a commotion and a lot of movement in the Khumbu Icefall. It was 6 a.m. The corpse was still being transported down. Fred, the Basecamp doctor, borrowed Moni's harness and crampons and left for the Icefall with Pem and Kami. The doctor returned to Basecamp about 4 p.m. Pem and Kami were a couple of hours behind him. The body was still in the Icefall near the last big set of stairs. Someone would have to go up again tomorrow to bring the corpse the rest of the way. Pem and Kami were drained from the exertion, ate early, and went straight to bed. Moni kept an emotional distance around the death to keep her focus on summiting. She busied herself with signing expedition forms and visiting with friends at the Mountain Madness Expedition tent. Even so, she was frightened by the incident, and dreamed about the accident that night.

The next day, early in the morning of May 3, there was more commotion in the Icefall. Finally, the body was delivered to Basecamp by Sherpas and members of the Parivar Expedition, the company hired by the deceased climber. Pem and Kami stayed in Basecamp to rest and pack for the Camp II climb the following morning.

When Pem and Kami stepped outside Moni's tent, they noticed that the lead Sherpa of the Parivar Expedition had clipped the sled and corpse to the exterior tent pole. Worried about ghosts and bad Karma, Pem and Kami performed a ritual before entering the tent where Moni was resting. They cleansed and sprinkled holy water on themselves and burned juniper to prevent the spirit from following them inside. Exchanging a quick nod, they agreed not to mention it to Moni.

Later that evening, near the Basecamp helipad, Moni noticed that the deceased climber's brother and a handful of foreigners had lit a fire and held a vigil by the corpse. Someone had put a khada over the body. Pem and Kami were relieved that the corpse had been moved away from their tent. The next morning, the corpse was flown to Kathmandu.

AVALANCHE

Expedition Day 39
May 4, 2005

At 5:30 a.m. the radio in Basecamp crackled again, followed by another urgent dispatch.

"Big avalanche hit Camp I. Camp I is gone. Repeat: Camp I gone."

Moni recognized Lhakpa Sherpa's voice, the Basecamp liaison. Still half asleep, she didn't take in the details of the call. In her foggy mind, she had imagined an avalanche on Pumori, Nuptse, or Lingtren, where avalanches were common and heard regularly, day and night. Pem and Kami had already left for Camp II to set up for their summit bid. As they unzipped the tent, she had sleepily said, "Goodbye. Be careful."

When Moni went to breakfast, their cook, Pemba dai, told her that Camp I was obliterated. "We don't know full damage yet," he said.

Moni reached Kami on the walkie-talkie. He and Pem arrived at Camp I after the avalanche.

"Camp I was a big pile of ice, rock, and snow and most of the tents were flattened," Kami told Moni.

Of the seventy tents in camp, only two were standing. Six were injured, he had heard, including a foreigner who was climbing without a permit. A flurry of calls crisscrossed the airwaves as expedition teams tried to account for team members. No one knew exactly how many climbers had slept in Camp I that night. Pem, Kami, and other Sherpas on site helped with rescue efforts. Pem told Moni to spread the word in Basecamp that the entire Camp was destroyed.

In the meantime, Moni's family had heard the news and were frantically trying to reach her. Although it was still snowing and the weather forecast called for continued snow over the next few days, some climbers who had left a tent at Camp I climbed up to look for their gear. Few were lucky enough to find their belongings.

By 3 p.m. the injured began flowing into Basecamp. Luckily, only a few climbers were in Camp I when the avalanche blasted through, and most injuries were not life threatening. One climbing Sherpa suffered a broken spine, however, and it took several Sherpas to carry him down to safety.

In Basecamp, Moni and a few others approached one of the injured climbers. He was from Poland, he said, and his face was badly damaged. When they realized that he was the illegal climber everyone had been talking about, Moni and the Basecamp liaison officers met in the dining hall to discuss a course of action. Concerned that the climber would sneak away in the night, they decided to take his passport and notify the Nepal Embassy. But when they approached his one-person tent and asked for his passport, he pretended not to understand. When an officer leaned in to search his body, he handed over his ID and tried to hide his passport in his underwear. The officer wrestled the passport away from him. The officers took his plane ticket, as well, and gave the climber food and tea before heading back to their own tents late that evening.

The next morning, a Royal Nepal Army helicopter landed in Basecamp to fly the corpse to Kathmandu. The Polish climber was still in camp and was fined $350 for climbing illegally.

Late in the morning, Moni received a package from her parents containing supplies the team needed for the remainder of the expedition: extra batteries, 10,000 rupees, wet wipes, crackers, three bottles of oxygen, fruits, vegetables, a pair of trousers, and one black jacket.

The past few days had been unsettling and disappointing to the climbers who had pitched tents at Camp I. All their provisions for a summit bid were lost, and they were headed home. Two discouraged climbers from the Parivar Expedition approached the Rotary team tent the evening of May 5. One climber's face was cut and bruised, the other had injured a hand. In the aftermath of the avalanche and one client's death, their 2005 expedition had ended. They hoped to come back next year with another expedition. Moni wrote down the names of a few expedition companies that she trusted and wished them good luck. The pair returned later with chocolates.

Throughout the week, helicopters flew in and out of Basecamp ferrying climbers back to Kathmandu. Despite the series of tragic events, the Rotary Nepal Centennial Everest Expedition team continued preparations for a summit bid and packed for a Camp II climb. The snowstorm was still raging, with the extended forecast showing a slight improvement and a weather break around May 8. Later that evening, they watched video clips of the Camp I avalanche destruction. Kami had recorded the scene and sold the videos to Nepal TV.

Expedition Day 42
May 8, 2005

The weather was finally improving. Pem, Kami, and Moni were sitting outside the kitchen tent reading newspapers and devouring cinnamon rolls while strategizing their move to Camp II when Pemba Dorje Sherpa, "Speed Pemba," stopped by. The nickname "Speed Pemba" had stuck after climbing from Basecamp to the summit in a record eight hours and ten minutes, a speed record that was later revoked by the Nepal Supreme Court for insufficient evidence. Speed Pemba stopped by to say that his team was moving to Camp II the next day, May 9. He offered the Rotary team an extra oxygen bottle to stash at Camp IV and handed Moni a spare regulator to use for summit day.

Later that evening, as the team was packing, Pem said, "Get ready. This time, we might go to summit from Camp II."

Camp II, also known as Advanced Basecamp, is sometimes used as a base for a summit bid. With that possibility in play, they packed everything they might need—flags, food, chocolate, batteries, camera, extra clothes, regulators, summit suit. From now to the rapidly approaching end of the Everest climbing season, their days would be intense—if the weather held, if their bodies held.

SUMMIT ATTEMPT

Expedition Day 43
May 9, 2005

The Rotary team arrived at "Crampon Point" at 6:30 a.m. and entered the Khumbu Icefall. The Khumbu Icefall had changed significantly since the last time they climbed and, to Moni, seemed more difficult. They arrived at Camp I just after noon and spent an hour resting and snacking on fried chicken and roti with their climbing friend, Maya. It was another 1.6 miles with a 1,500-foot elevation gain to Camp II, a few more hours of climbing.

At 3:30 p.m., they reached the last set of tall ladders before the Western Cwm. While they rested, Kami rummaged through his pack and broke out a can of Pringles and juice. He smiled at Moni, handing her the whole cannister of chips, her favorite. They talked about Michiri, wondering if she would get a permit. With Michiri gone, the expedition might feel slightly less stressful.

They made Camp II at 4:30 p.m. Hoping to prevent an altitude headache, Moni drank five liters of water and devoured as much food as possible, despite her lack of hunger. Pem and Kami rested and planned their climb to Camp IV, preparing to leave the next day at 2 a.m. It would be a difficult climb with the remaining gear they had to carry to set up camp, and they needed to get up and down quickly.

Through the night, Moni had trouble sleeping. After drinking so much water, she had to pee frequently, which meant rustling around the tent for the "pee bottle." Going to the bathroom outside in extreme weather and on a slope in darkness is treacherous, so climbers usually stay inside the tent and pee into a wide-mouthed bottle that's emptied outside in the morning. Having to defecate in the middle of the night, especially in a down summit suit, is more problematic. Given the offensive smell to tent mates, pooping inside the tent is discouraged. Stepping out to "go" has led to tragic accidents. Although climbers have a fixed rope just outside their tent, sometimes, out of sleepiness or high-altitude confusion, they forget to clip in. Raging winds or a sudden gust can push a climber off a cliff or down a slope. Climbing out in tent slippers will send one sliding down a steep, icy slope toward death.

Early on the morning of May 10, Pem and Kami departed for Camp IV. The climb from Camp II (21,000 feet) to Camp IV (26,625 feet) covers 5,000 feet in elevation and crosses into the Death Zone where most climbers require supplemental oxygen. Near Camp III, strong, gusty winds forced them back. This section of the climb is notorious for its treacherous weather conditions, with winds whipping across the South Col between Everest and Lhotse at 60 mph or higher.

Late morning, a cook from another expedition notified Moni that Pem and Kami were on their way back and would be arriving back at Camp II around noon. She prepared tea for them and alerted their cook, Pemba dai, to have a meal prepared. Upon arrival, Pem climbed into the tent and flopped onto a sleeping bag, exhausted from the climb. The oxygen cannisters he and Kami had carried up weeks earlier were now buried in snow. The last few days had been stormy, but they hadn't expected that much snow, and despite digging frantically, had come up empty-handed. Tired and sweaty, they gave up the search and grew concerned.

"We worried we wouldn't find them," Pem said. He wondered if they had been stolen. "It happens at Everest," he said. "People sometimes steal the bottles and sell them. One small bottle of oxygen costs $450."

Without a full supply of oxygen for each team member, their climb would be over. Since the Rotary had reduced their funding from $70,000 to $40,000 because of the tsunami in Thailand, the team didn't have the funds to buy replacements.

On an earlier climb, Pem had retrieved one tank, but the others were nowhere to be found. To keep their expedition alive, they needed help. The team called the foreign ministry and secured permit fee waivers, and the Nepal Rotarians found a hotel that would donate a tent and more oxygen tanks. Because they couldn't afford to hire their own team to fix ropes to reach the summit, they would have to follow another team. This would make them entirely dependent on another expedition's judgment, schedule, and pacing, but they had no choice if they wanted to make a summit bid this year.

The next day, word in camp was that a group of climbers planned to summit on May 16 and 18. To avoid the crowd and a wait in a long, snaking queue to the summit, the Rotary team targeted May 18 to summit.

"Everyone wants to get to the top first, and the trail gets jammed in the bottleneck areas where passing is impossible," Pem said.

The wait forces climbers to stay in the Death Zone far longer, increasing the risk of high-altitude sickness and death.

Now, it was a race against time and weather to get set up at Camp IV. On May 11, Pem and Moni planned to hike to Camp III, while Kami took a rest day in Camp II, but Moni had another debilitating altitude headache. The team decided to wait until 7 a.m. to see if she was well enough to move higher. Pem boiled water and made soup.

"You need to get stronger," he said, handing Moni a cup of hot soup. "You can do this, Moni. I know you can," he urged.

After taking Diamox and feeling no improvement, Moni went to bed. Another change of plans. Pem would leave for Camp IV in the morning and descend back to Camp III to search for the missing oxygen bottle while Kami and Moni climbed up to Camp III. Moni hadn't fully acclimated at Camp III altitude yet. An hour later, Moni and Kami packed helmets, juice, hot water, and Pringles and set out. Moni again had difficulty getting to the higher Camps. Each step was slow and arduous, Moni said.

"At Camp II, I took three steps, then a one-minute rest, another step, then a breath and rest."

Her whole mind was entirely focused on taking another step.

Halfway to Camp III, they ran into Pem descending back to Camp II. He was worn out and walking stiffly. His back hurt, but he was jubilant. After more digging, he had found the missing oxygen tanks.

The three returned to Camp II together and rested. On the way back to their tent, they stopped by the Asian Trekking Expedition to ask Speed Pemba if the Rotary team could use one of their tents already set up in Camp IV. It was a common courtesy for climbers to let those they knew and trusted utilize unoccupied tents. It alleviated the brutal trek up through the Death Zone with heavy gear. Pem was fairly certain Speed Pemba would offer his tent if it wasn't in use, but he was down at Basecamp and Pem was unable to reach him.

The next day, Kami and a few other Sherpas planned to overnight at Camp III and climb to Camp IV to set up for a summit bid while Moni completed her Camp III acclimatization rotation.

Expedition Day 46
May 12, 2005

Pem began the climb to Camp IV at 2 a.m. The forecast was for continued high winds on the steep, exposed terrain, so Kami slept in and would catch up with Pem after dropping Moni off at Camp III. The altitude at Camp II had gotten to Moni again. She woke up tired and frustrated with a nasty headache and diarrhea. "Now, I'm getting really irritated with my head!" she wrote in her journal.

Basecamp was glamourous compared to Camp II, Moni thought. The tents were crowded together, there was no toilet, and drinking water was made from melted snow and ice scraped from the ground near their tent. Moni worried that whatever bacteria was in the water was causing her to feel sick. She tried to sleep off the headache, called down to Basecamp from her walkie-talkie, and listened to FM radio. She was eating a lunch of a fruit snack, *titaura,* and prawns and apple juice when a Sherpa with another expedition came to the tent, asking if he could use their gas to boil water. He had run out. Moni melted water for him and filled his thermos. About twenty minutes later, he was back with a Sherpa friend looking for medical tape. His friend had taken a fall and his eyeglasses had smashed into his face, leaving a gaping wound. Moni gave them tape and advised the injured Sherpa to descend and see the Basecamp doctor.

Kami had caught up with Pem, but again it was too windy to make Camp IV. The two of them, plus a few other Sherpas, climbed back down and arrived at Camp II at 6:30 p.m. Kami had caught a cold and bad cough.

"I was always getting a cough and cold like everyone else," Kami said.

His strategy was to sleep it off and keep climbing.

The rumor from down at Basecamp was that Michiri had gotten her summit permit and that she was planning to climb without a Sherpa. Moni's anger rose like a fast-moving cloud. "Who did she think she was, climbing alone?" she debated furiously in her journal.

The next day, Pem, Kami, and Moni would climb back down to Basecamp to recover from their illnesses. Moni still had not completed her acclimatization rotation by spending a night at Camp III where she would start supplemental oxygen, but at this point, they all agreed she might have to pass over that rotation.

"Many climbers were skipping the overnight there," Pem said.

The prevailing medical theory in 2005 was that it was unnecessary and too dangerous to overnight at Camp III, the toll on the body too great.

Once again, the team settled back into Basecamp to wait. The fixed ropes from Camp IV to the summit still had to be set before anyone could make a summit bid, but bad weather had prevented their installation. If the prevailing weather pattern refused to break, all the climbers would run out of time. The season would be shut down by government mandate at the end of May, or by monsoons, which would drench the Himalaya and cause the Khumbu Icefall to crumble any day now.

Expedition Day 48
May 14 - 15, 2005

On Saturday, the storm clouds parted, producing a remarkably clear and calm day on Everest. A weather window opened for yet another historic first: for the first time in history, a helicopter landed and took off from the summit.

Until then, weather, altitude, cold temperatures, the updraft and downdrafts, and lack of visual cues for landing had rendered rescue attempts at the top of the world unattainable. Updrafts at Everest's summit have enough force to push a helicopter away as soon it sets down. Defying the turbulent environment and the impossible, Didier Delsalle, a French Air Force fighter pilot, search and rescue operator, and helicopter test pilot, landed on the small patch of rock and ice that constitutes the south summit in a stripped-down, lighter version of a Eurocopter AS350 B3. The Eurocopter Squirrel is certified to operate at a maximum of 23,000 feet. Acquiring civil aviation clearance to land on Everest and transporting the helicopter was itself an Olympic challenge. The helicopter parts were flown by cargo plane to India for reassembly in a hangar that was nearly destroyed by a sandstorm. In a lucky break, the helicopter was spared. In early May, Delsalle flew the reassembled helicopter to Lukla and on recon missions around the summit. While practicing the approach, Delsalle discovered a consequential problem. On the updraft side of the summit, the helicopter would still be climbing as it landed, even if he took all the power out of the aircraft. On the downdraft side of the summit, the aircraft would be going backward. The helicopter didn't have enough power to counter these effects, so if he was going to set a record and stick the skids on Everest's south summit, he would have to fly skillfully and smoothly between the updrafts and downdrafts in 65 mph winds. In addition, he'd have to fly with his windows open to prevent the interior windshield from icing up in the extreme cold. It was minus 25 degrees Fahrenheit at the summit that day. Delsalle would also have to ensure that the rotor wash did not jeopardize any climbers or blow them off the mountain.

On May 13, Delsalle landed on the summit and stayed for almost four minutes, but later discovered that his camera hadn't recorded the landing. Setting a world record required proof and the Nepali government demanded it, or no record. Most climbers had gone down to Basecamp in the storm, and it would take them two days to summit. On May 14, he landed a second time as a small group of climbers neared the top.

From Camp II, Pem and Kami saw the helicopter nose around toward the summit.

"It was quite a show," Pem said, although a puzzling one. No one knew about the planned attempt, which prompted a steady stream of calls to Nepalese authorities and much speculation.

Back at Basecamp, as they continued to recover, both Moni and Kami had developed a case of the Khumbu cough—a persistent dry cough caused by the cold, dry air at high altitudes, a common problem for Everest climbers who stay at high altitudes for lengthy periods of time. Doctors believe that the combination of exertion, sub-zero temperatures, and low humidity dries out the lung lining and bronchi. At Basecamp, with sleep restored, headaches gone, and appetites returning, they were supposed to feel physically healthy again for a summit bid.

With all the delays and the summit window rapidly closing, Moni's frustrations grew, and her mental state began to deteriorate. Things that were out of their control didn't bother Pem and Kami. They were comfortable with all the waiting around and shifting plans, but Moni was eager to get off the mountain. She felt uncharacteristically out of sorts and angry.

"I don't know what happened to me," she said. "I was bad-tempered and scolded Dendi, our kitchen boy, because he didn't prepare tea when he knew we had a guest coming."

The previous day, Moni was angry with Pem for playing cards instead of joining her at the Asian Trekking cook tent. Her dream for the most perilous prize—Everest's summit—was rapidly eroding.

Expedition Day 52
May 18, 2005

Finally, the day had arrived, they thought. After months of training, the Rotary team left for Everest's summit with high hopes of setting a record or two. They rose at 5 a.m., ate a hearty breakfast, gave a brief interview to reporters, and started for the Icefall. They made it through without a mishap. At the last long ladder before the Western Cwm and Camp II, Moni realized that she had forgotten to drink water during the climb and was feeling dehydrated and depleted. Pem climbed ahead to Camp II, got the stove going and melted snow to have fresh water available when she arrived. Moni reached Camp II at 4 p.m.

Kami stayed behind at Camp I and would follow, climbing to Camp II as Pem and Moni ascended to Camp III. After resting, Pem and Moni walked over to Wonghu Sherpa's tent, where they had a meal and talked into the evening. The subject of Michiri came up. She had not reached Camp III, someone reported, and had returned to Basecamp due to a severely swollen face.

SUMMIT PUSH

Expedition Day 53 - 55
May 19 - 25, 2005

On Thursday, May 19, the team was awakened at 5 a.m. by the scurrying sound of footsteps rushing around Camp II. A group of climbers were leaving for Camp III in anticipation of a May 21 summit. The Rotary team prepared to climb, but at 6 a.m. Kami learned that Speed Pemba's team was heading up the mountain and their Camp IV expedition tent would be unavailable. They agreed to postpone their summit bid until May 22. Upon hearing the news, Moni felt sick. After fifty-four days on the mountain, the crucial day had arrived, and this felt like a devastating set back. This meant Michiri would likely reach the summit before her, shattering one of the team's record-breaking goals. Discouraged, they all crawled back into their sleeping bags.

The following day, May 20, Pem, Kami, and Moni rose before dawn, ate a quick breakfast of cornflakes, Kellogg's Chocos, and tea, then shouldered their backpacks, this time, stuffed with summit gear—flags, oxygen, harness, ice axe, food, batteries, clothing, and the Canon camera. Moni was expecting her menstrual cycle again soon and took medication to delay its onset to eliminate any chance of symptoms during the summit bid.

The team departed Camp II at 5:30 a.m. and by 7:30 a.m. they were climbing toward Camp III. Kami had climbed ahead. To avoid lugging their bulky summit suits, Moni and Pem put them on near Camp II. By 10 a.m., though, the sun was already beating down, making them miserably hot and uncomfortable. In her journal, Moni wrote about her frustration: "I had sport boots that didn't fit right, crampons, and a heavy bag, and I was extremely hot. At one point, I lost my temper & kicked my backpack."

It was another slow slog up the steep slope of the Lhotse face while clipped into fixed ropes. Even with crampons, it was difficult to get a foothold in the compact ice, but the jumars helped them ascend. Although the safety ropes had been set in place recently and checked, it was hard to trust those thin ropes, especially in congested places.

"I worried in places where twenty climbers hung from the ropes at the same time," Pem said.

Halfway up, well before Camp III, the wind kicked up and the mild, overcast day with its steely, granite skies turned to snow. Wind and ice hammered at their faces. While hanging on the fixed rope on the steepest section of the trail, with Pem and a Korean climber just ahead of her and another Korean climber directly behind her, Moni was struck with an urgent, unwelcome feeling. *Oh no, not now!* she thought. Her stomach rumbled and began to churn. It felt like someone had put a lead weight in her stomach. Then the sharp pains came.

Dangling from the ropes, she hollered up to Pem, "I have diarrhea," with horror and disbelief that this was happening where there was no way to be discreet. "Of all days, why today?" she asked out loud.

"Climb a little higher," Pem yelled down. "There is one place to stop on the ice."

But holding it was not an option. "I can't wait. I have to do it here," Moni shouted back.

It was one of those weirdly awkward situations – harnessed and clipped into the safety lines, how do you drop a summit suit flap fast? Moni swung around, wedged her crampons into the ice, and with some wiggling around, unfastened her drop seat and let it go. She hoped she wouldn't spin on the fixed ropes and make a mess in her suit or on the climber below.

"From behind, I must have looked funny," Moni recalled, laughing.

"You get used to the lack of privacy pretty quickly after a few days in Basecamp," Pem said. Even so, there's a bit of an internal shock factor to an urgent and public nature call.

By 4:30 p.m. on May 21, they had reached the lower part of Camp III and the first set of tents that pitched awkwardly downslope. Moni was so tired she couldn't make it to their expedition tent, which was another hour and a half further upslope. They stopped there and crawled into Speed Pemba's empty tent. With the little energy he had in reserve, Pem climbed to their camp above and brought down food, oxygen, and gas for the stove. Pem considers himself a steady climber, but not fast and strong like Kami and most of his Sherpa friends. That day, he found it exhausting to climb up and carry supplies back down. For dinner, they ate rara soup, *chapati*, *aloo* and *masu*, and then went straight to bed to rest for the next day's climb to Camp IV. About 4 a.m., Moni woke up feeling uneasy. She took a hit of oxygen, but that left her feeling more agitated.

The following day, the Rotary team was dealt another blow that scuttled plans to make Camp IV, the last stop before the big summit push. Climbers who had gone up expecting to summit on May 21 were met with high winds and snow and were on their way back down to Camp III.

"We were a little confused about what to do next," Moni said. Pem called down to Camp II and EBC to get the weather forecast. Bad news. Whipping wind and snow would prohibit a summit attempt on May 22. The subtropical jet stream—atmospheric highways in the upper troposphere where winds can blow 80 to 275 mph—would not relent for at least a couple of days. Climbers can withstand winds of about 30 mph, but beyond that, can be swiftly blown off the mountain.

Historically, mid-May has been the best time to summit during the spring climbing season. About that time, the polar- front jet stream drifts north, causing the subtropical jet stream's icy winds to relax. But as weather patterns go, they are rarely consistent. In 2018, the jet stream was off the summit and winds quieted for a rare eleven days straight. In contrast, in mid-April 2019, when storms typically diminish in the Bay of Bengal and create a period of good weather, Cyclone Fani blew through Everest, causing delays in rope-setting and very few opportunities to summit. Small weather windows of only three consecutive days of diminished winds opened, putting immense pressure on an over-crowded 2019 season that saw eleven deaths.

The morning of May 22, in blustery snow and wind, Pem and Moni clipped into the fixed ropes and started their descent to Camp II, with Pem climbing slightly ahead of Moni. Kami was still higher up the mountain. The Lhotse Face ice wall was surprisingly icy that day and required skillful crampon technique. A few minutes into the descent, Pem told Moni he felt sick.

"It's your turn for diarrhea," she said, laughing.

About an hour into the descent, Moni screamed. She had flipped upside down and dropped down the ice wall so fast it seemed as if someone or something was villainously pulling her down. The rope twitched and jerked to a halt when her safety line caught. Upside down and disoriented with her backpack glued to the ice wall, she could hardly move.

"I almost died," Moni recalled. "The pitch was so steep, you could slide all the way down to Camp II."

Although safety anchors are screwed into the ice every 15 to 20 feet on the steepest sections of the ice wall, climbers can still be injured in a fall.

Pem was a short distance ahead but didn't hear the commotion. A Russian climber behind Moni quickly descended to assist. With his aid, she was able to right herself and wedge her crampons into the ice and get back on the route. Again, Moni was furious with Pem for being so far ahead that he couldn't offer help—maybe even save her from injury or death. He had lost his ice axe earlier in the day and now she felt that he was being irresponsible. Later, she would acknowledge that her anger was out of fear.

"You're so tired up there that small things irritate you. Your mind feels different. You feel sensitive, very low at times. You just want to sleep and not think about anything," she said. "When these dangerous things happen, your brain is in fight or flight even though the brain is slow."

Moni knew it wasn't healthy to be in such an aggressive, frustrated psychological place while climbing Everest because it could affect her safety and that of her team. She knew Pem was a good man, but in that oxygen-deprived moment, she felt he was lacking in certain attentive qualities.

"Pem is caring," she said, "but doesn't have a paying attention nature."

The dynamics of Pem and Moni's relationship were sometimes challenging. Pem knows that Moni dislikes being told she can't do something, or that she has to do things a certain way. He knows she gets irritated when she hasn't done something as well as someone else—like her competitor, Michiri—and will work hard to accomplish whatever outcome she's trying to achieve but will do it on her own terms. And he knows there's a little bit of a daredevil in her. Like an athletic coach, Pem tried to use those qualities to motivate her. Sometimes it worked, he said, but more often it backfired.

After studying the weather forecasts, Pem and Kami predicted the next weather window would be May 26 or 27. The team agreed that Pem and Kami would move down to Basecamp while Moni stayed in Camp II. This way, she would avoid crossing the Khumbu Icefall again in five days. In the warming spring sun, the Icefall was getting increasingly unpredictable with anchors starting to pull out, ladders slipping, and seracs moving more than usual. Plus, if the jet stream moved out earlier, Moni could conserve energy by starting the climb at Camp II. Pem and Kami could make it to Camp II quickly if they were rested and feeling well.

Alone at Camp II, Moni was bored and lonely at first. She slept a lot but finally found a routine, busying herself with tent-cleaning, rechecking her summit pack, and socializing with Wongchu's Peak Promotion expedition and two Korean expeditions. The Korean teams were among those who had attempted the summit the night of May 21, but were forced back. Now, like everyone else, they were reassessing, deciding whether to reposition for another summit bid or go home.

While she was reorganizing the tent, Moni's father called on the SAT phone to get an update.

"Things are going well," she said, "but the weather is a problem."

She knew in her heart that this would be her only chance to summit Everest. "If not this year, NO MORE SUMMIT!" she wrote in her journal on May 22. She did not share with her parents the rumor that no one would summit this late in the season. Meanwhile, down at Basecamp, Pem and Kami rested in anticipation of at least one more summit bid.

The next morning, May 22, there was extensive clatter and commotion around Camp II. A large group of climbers were packing up all their gear and heading for EBC. Their expeditions were ending without having achieved the holy grail. *This is unusual*, Moni thought. *The season typically ends late May, but here we are May 22, still waiting to summit. Would the Nepali government extend the season or shut it down?* she wondered. At noon she called down to Basecamp to check in with Pem.

"Come down," he said. "Kami and I will meet you at the tall ladder at the top of the Icefall."

Pem's voice sounded low and brooding Moni thought, unusual for the normally optimistic Pem.

That evening, Moni packed up to be ready for an early morning descent to reach the Icefall before it got late. She had spent most of the day talking to other climbers, including a Portuguese climber who had just climbed Lhotse. She noticed that he was missing part of his nose and a finger, lost to frostbite a few years earlier on a climbing expedition. He was heading home now and giving away some of his climbing gear. He tossed Moni a Nalgene water bottle.

The next morning, Camp II practically emptied out as they all headed down to Basecamp. On the way down, they met a group of climbers from the Mountain Madness Expedition waiting out the weather by practicing crevasse rescue training. Pem and Kami met Moni at the top of the Icefall as planned. By the time the three arrived in Basecamp, a celebratory atmosphere had taken over the tent city, with a lot of dancing and partying by the climbers whose expeditions had come to an end. It was May 23, and although these climbers never made the summit, they celebrated their personal achievements and were glad to be going home where they would recover physically and emotionally, remembering the climbing season for its unpredictable weather, the high winds and late fixing of ropes, and a helicopter landing on the summit. Once home, some would continue training and planning for next year's summit attempt. For others, it was the end of a dream.

The Rotary Nepal Centennial Everest Expedition team and a handful of others weren't ready to call it quits just yet. They were healthy enough and had enough supplies and faith to wait for favorable weather conditions. They would head back up to Camp II on May 26 unless the Nepali government shut down the season.

Expedition Day 60
May 26, 2005

The team rose at 5 a.m. Moni felt sick to her stomach again but pushed herself to keep going. Gastrointestinal issues remain a persistent problem at Basecamp no matter how long you've acclimatized.

After a brief interview with reporters at Basecamp, Kami and Moni left for Camp II, along with the group of remaining climbers. Pem stayed at EBC and would rejoin them at Camp II or III. In the middle of the night, a thunder and lightning storm rolled through, producing avalanches and treacherously slippery climbing conditions which delayed their Camp III ascent again.

Expedition Day 62
May 28, 2005

It was a cold morning on the mountain. Moni and Kami were up again at 5 a.m. but delayed climbing for several hours. About the time they were heading out, a large group had begun their ascent to Camp III, just ahead of them. They would lose energy and risk frostbite if they got caught up in a human traffic jam along the route or at Camp III.

It was a slow, seven-hour burning climb. By 5 p.m., Moni and Kami had settled into a tent borrowed from the Asian Trekking Expedition. Moni began supplemental oxygen at a low flow rate of 1 liter per minute, hoping it would give her physical strength and preserve cognitive function for the Camp IV climb. At the very least, supplemental oxygen could help reduce the risk of high-altitude pulmonary edema and keep the body warmer. Kami was having problems sleeping, so he started up on supplemental oxygen as well.

Summit Bid
May 29, 2005

When they woke up the following morning, the wind was shrieking outside their tent. A long, hard day loomed ahead. Once the team reached Camp IV, they would rest until 11 p.m. and then try for the summit, climbing in the dark with headlamps. If they hadn't reached the summit by 2 p.m., they would have to turn around to catch the last of the daylight before conditions turned against them. At the summit, they would only stay a few minutes, just long enough to take in the view and snap photos, then descend as quickly as possible. It would take six to ten hours to summit and at least half that time to descend back to Camp IV.

Moni and Kami started for Camp IV at 8:30 a.m. Kami climbed ahead with his usual quickness while Moni went at a slower pace, knowing that Pem soon would catch up. But he was climbing a little slower than usual that day, Moni noticed, perhaps due to a heavy pack and the steepness. Eventually, he caught up to Moni and they climbed together to the Geneva Spur, where Moni changed out her oxygen tank.

The Geneva Spur, at an elevation of 25,000 feet, is a steep, sharp-edged mass of ice and rock above the Lhotse Face and below the South Col, one of the last major obstacles before Camp IV. It's always windy in the horseshoe-shaped arc between Everest and Lhotse. The spur is so steep that climbers line up single file along the fixed ropes. To try and pass anyone there would be a death wish. A tangle of old and new ropes crisscrossed the spur. Despite the "leave no trace behind" policy, the reality is that climbers are too tired or ill to cut or clean up the ropes after a summit climb and leave them to rot or be disposed of on a future clean-up Everest day.

"You have to find the new line or just grab a bunch and pray," Pem said.

Once over the Geneva Spur, Pem and Moni appreciated the little bit of relief on the flatter traverse just below the South Col and Camp IV. By the time Moni and Pem arrived in camp at 7:30 p.m., Kami was already resting.

They were tired after the ascent, especially Moni after twelve hours of climbing, and they only had a few hours of rest before starting the summit bid departure at 10 p.m. As soon as Pem and Moni reached the tent, they repacked for the summit, lightening their loads to the essentials, checking and double-checking their gear. They checked batteries in their headlamps, phone, and cameras, sorted gear, and tucked items that needed to stay warm into their sleeping bags. The oxygen tanks were packed last. Then they ate and drank enough to get them through the night climb that would begin in a few hours, as well as the descent. Crammed into the tent like sardines, masked up with three oxygen tanks and gear bags between them, they tried to sleep until time to go.

While Pem and Kami slept, Moni lay awake. Her mind raced. She worried about whether she could reach the summit given their late arrival and short rest before the night climb. Her pace was slower than Kami and Pem. Would she be able to maintain a pace that got her to the top and kept her warm enough during the night climb? She thought about Michiri beating her to the top and couldn't shake off the intrusive thoughts. They'd heard that Michiri reached Camp IV at 1 p.m. that day, way ahead of Moni and Pem. The voices of climbers in Basecamp praising Michiri's strength played back in Moni's mind. *Wow, Michiri is strong. Michiri climbs like a Sherpa.*

"They automatically thought Michiri would summit, and I wouldn't," Moni recalled.

It was extremely cold that night. At 11:40 p.m., Kami stood outside the tent, his gear bag on his back, crampons strapped on, and headlamp turned on bright. He felt a little edgy.

"We're already late to start," he said, hurrying his teammates along, gasping between coughs. Kami had the dreaded, rib-breaking Khumbu cough from the dry, cold air.

Normally, climbers start the summit bid around 8 or 9 p.m., or about two hours after the rope fixers set the ropes. This timing allows climbers to avoid waiting in the dark, highly susceptible to frostbite and hypothermia, in a long and slow-moving line of climbers who are clipped into fixed ropes and sucking down precious oxygen reserves. But that night, the rope fixers were delayed and didn't start setting the route until 10 p.m. Ideally, climbers want to reach the summit by 8 or 9 a.m. and no later than early afternoon to give them ample time for the descent, especially if they encounter problems. Descending Everest is considered the most dangerous part of the climb.

The climb from Camp IV to Everest's summit is one of the most physically and technically demanding climbs of an Everest expedition. It's about 1.7 miles of steep climbing on a fixed-line rope on the section of the mountain where acclimatization is meaningless. At this altitude, the body uses oxygen faster than it can replenish and thus can never acclimatize, even with supplemental oxygen. Staying too long will kill you.

Climbing together in a single-file line, they dug the toes of their crampons into the hardpacked ice and pulled their way up toward Camp IV slowly and repetitively with the jumars, taking in oxygen at about 3.5 liters per minute. Normal flow rates average between 0.5 and 1 liter per minute while sleeping and 2 to 3 liters per minute when climbing above 26,000 feet, but because oxygen tanks are heavy and expensive, flow rates are kept as low as possible. This section of the climb, made mostly in the dark, typically takes seven or more hours, and in this final steep section, the goal is to remain slow and steady, keeping the heart rate low while breathing in oxygen.

Two hours into the climb, Moni's pace had slowed to a crawl. She knew that Michiri was ahead of her, but at this point, she could no longer afford to care. The route was so steep, the air so thin, and the trail so dark that, for safety, she had to focus intensely on each step and control her breathing. Mentally and physically, she could not climb any faster. Halfway into the climb, Pem and Kami realized they had a critical decision to make.

"The pace is too slow to summit by noon. We won't make it," Pem said.

If they summited past noon, there wasn't enough time to get down safely.

"Let's send Kami ahead with the flag," Moni said.

Feeling strong and still climbing fast, Kami Sherpa was their best chance at getting the Rotary flag to the summit.

As Kami climbed ahead, Pem and Moni crept slowly toward the summit, overtaking climbers one by one. When they got to the Balcony, a series of snow-covered benches on the southeast ridge of Everest, Moni couldn't believe her eyes. Just ahead, Michiri was lying in the snow, obviously struggling to breathe. She was arguing with her Sherpa guide, insisting on continuing up, insinuating that it would be his fault if she didn't summit.

"If you want to live, descend, now," her guide implored fiercely.

Michiri's guide had seen this before. The climber's mind, once filled with optimism and big dreams of standing on the summit, becomes crudely occupied with one thing: taking the next step. Each painfully slow gain turns increasingly grueling and exacting until unrecognizable as a gain. The climber sits, unmoved, on Sagamartha—this dazzling, breath-taking, life-taking, wind-scoured glacial mountain of the gods, and thinks in contradiction, *"I will make it,"* and *"This is not how I want to die."* Any climber, no matter how fit or trained, could be left to shrivel and freeze in the stone tower of Everest. For every six successful summits, one climber will die.

Shortly after Pem and Moni passed Michiri, Kami stood on the summit and planted the Rotary flag in the ice. He had just finished taking photos and was about to descend when the radio buzzed. It was Pem.

"We are fifteen minutes from summit. Can you wait?"

Disbelieving what he heard, Kami looked down the mountain and could just make out two climbers slowly ascending. Passing Michiri had lit a fire under Moni!

At 11 a.m. the Rotary team circled together in celebration at the top of the world.

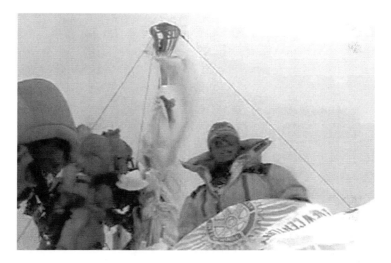

Photo credit: Kami Sherpa

FOR BETTER OR WORSE
AT 29,035 FEET

Photo credit: Kami Sherpa

Expedition Day 64
May 30, 2005

Up in the stratosphere, approaching the stars, on a narrow slab of slanting rock and ice about the size of a small car, the Rotary Nepal Centennial Everest Expedition team stood euphorically on Everest's summit taking in the view—a view of infinite indigo and white horizons within the blue curvature of the earth, a sea of clouds and bone-white peaks stretching across Nepal and the Tibetan Plateau. At last, on the sixty-fourth day of the expedition, their luck had turned.

On the summit, the temperature bore out a punishing minus 40 degrees Fahrenheit. It was one of the last few good-weather days before the god of winds unleashed a 65-mph wind and the Indian monsoon reversed, pounding Everest with rain, wind, and snow.

Everest's small, narrow summit can only hold five or six climbers at a time. Ordinarily, climbers stay only ten to twenty minutes, just enough time to take in the view, celebrate, and snap a photo. The summit is no place to linger. Getting down as quickly as possible before the body fails, and to preserve enough oxygen for the descent, is imperative. Tragedies take place on the summit. Inattention or sluggishness induced by the elevation kills. One foot planted too close to the edge, a crampon becoming tangled in the prayer flags, or a sudden gust can result in death.

Straddling their native country and Tibet, ignoring the fierce wind robbing them of body warmth and threatening to blow them off the mountain, Moni and Pem removed their packs and sat on the snow-covered summit. Just above them, a tattered tangle of prayer flags and khadas placed by Sherpas streamed down from Everest's highest point.

Kami stood beside his teammates leaning forward, bracing against the pitch and howling crosswind. Overwhelmed with joy and excitement but exhausted from the sixteen-hour summit ascent, riding on pure adrenaline, the three climbers stood together on the summit holding the Rotary flag and posed for a photograph. Moni spoke into Kami's video camera while tightly clutching a family photograph to keep it from blowing into Tibet. Triumphant and breathless, she addressed the Nepal Rotary and thanked sponsors. Her words came in short, halting gasps and were quickly swept by the wind, evaporating into thin air. She had memorized a prepared speech and written the words on paper in case her memory was hijacked by the high altitude—a problem experienced climbers had warned her about.

> *"Hello from Everest's Summit! Pem, Kami, and I have reached the top of the world and hoisted the Rotary Centennial Flag ... On behalf of all the Rotarians of Nepal, we want to make a statement: Let there be peace and harmony around the globe and let people live like human beings and share brotherhood. Let this message be carried to the youths of society so that they can play a positive role since they are the caretakers of tomorrow...*
>
> *We thank all the Rotarians and the members of the Rotary Nepal organizing committee for the moral boost and for helping us make this expedition a success. We thank our sponsors for helping us financially, the organizing committee for helping us realize our dreams, and our parents for believing in us. Thanks, Rotary Nepal.*
>
> *—excerpt from the journal of Moni Mulepati*

Kami had been on the summit for more than thirty minutes, and although not usually inclined to worry, he was eager to climb down to safety. The team still had the problem of descent and the acceleration of catastrophe the longer they waited. Their oxygen masks were on and off their faces while they were on the summit, their supplies waning.

After Moni finished her recorded speech, she stepped closer to Pem, tapped him on the arm and gave him a look of expectancy, her eyes squinted, brows lifted. Pem stared back, a puzzled look on his face. The altitude seemed to have erased his memory.

"Pem, hurry," she gasped. "Find the garland and vermillion powder. We're getting married."

Startled by his forgetfulness, Pem flew into action. He kneeled on the hard snow and rummaged deep in his pack. Moni tore into her backpack, looking for something. As Kami stuffed the rotary flag into his backpack, he studied his teammates with confusion. Why were they both unpacking? They had been on the summit longer than expected and should have been descending.

From the very bottom of his gear bag, Pem yanked out the two *Dubo ko Malas* and the vermillion powder he had secretly stowed when they left Kathmandu in March. Then Kami caught on. In Hindu tradition, a bride and groom drape these garlands around each other's neck as a symbol of everlasting love. The Dubo, made of Bermuda grass which stays vibrant long after harvesting, blesses newlyweds with fertility and prosperity in their married life. Moni pulled out a Newari *haku patasi*, a traditional sari with a red border, from her pack and wrapped it around her body, transforming her summit suit into a wedding dress.

Although Kami knew they were in love, he was completely shocked. As a new group of westerners squeezed by them and wedged themselves on the summit, Kami looked directly at Pem and Moni and said, "Are you serious?"

He grabbed his video camera and began recording his teammates making another mark on history: the first wedding on top of the world. Pem and Moni removed their oxygen masks, unzipped their summit suits to the collarbone, and slipped a mala around each other's neck. Smiling, Pem removed his gloves and rubbed a thumb in vermillion powder, first tossing powder over his shoulder four times for good measure, then smudging Moni's forehead with a red dot. Moni reciprocated, placing a vermillion circle on Pem's forehead with a gloved hand. They stared into each other's eyes, their sober expressions and nervous laughs revealing the weight of their actions. Pem hesitated as if, in his oxygen-deprived state, he'd forgotten something else or had changed his mind, then grinned and planted a kiss on Moni's cheek. Shyly, she smiled and looked away.

As the wind blasted a plume of snow and ice crystals off the summit, Kami offered the couple a blessing and took photos. Moni pulled out a formal marriage document and collected signatures from the handful of foreigners who shared the summit.

Pem suddenly remembered the Canon camera stashed in his pack and the $100,000 sponsorship. With cold, numb fingers, he struggled to take photos and fulfill their contract. The camera didn't work, and later he would realize he had forgotten to install the battery, which was tucked in an inside pocket of his summit suit for warmth.

After the wedding, Moni called Rotary members and her family to share the news.

"Dad, we are on the top. I summited!"

"I won't believe it until you come down safely," he responded before Shanti snatched the phone away. The phone passed swiftly around the Mulepati family for congratulations.

"We have to go. Put Aunty Vijaya on the phone," Moni said. "Aunty, there is another bit of good news," she panted. "Pem and I got married on top. Now, convince Dad and Mom it's okay or I'm not coming home." *Click.*

Moni hung up before Aunty could respond. As soon as the call ended, a feeling of dread blazed through Moni. As the Newari saying goes, did she just cut off the nose of her father? If a girl brings shame to her father or the family, it is said that she has cut off her father's nose or lowered her father's head in shame.

"At first, I was totally motivated," Moni said. "But once I told Aunty, then I got scared. What if they abandoned me?"

Moni always had it in her heart to make her father and family proud. There was nothing malicious in her decision to marry Pem. Her parents liked Pem. If they summited Everest and set a world record, she thought they would embrace their union. But standing on the top of Everest, about to begin the dangerous descent to Camp IV, her heart sank, and she wasn't so sure. As she climbed down, doubt seeped in. She thought about all the times she questioned whether she should marry Pem.

"When I was walking slowly by myself, I thought a lot, *should I marry this guy?* When I was walking in the scary Icefall, and the time I fell, I thought I might *not* want to marry this guy!"

Following her own song of love instead of tradition could cost Moni everything. Once again, she felt the weight of what it meant for a Newari woman to marry outside her caste, to make a life-changing decision without familial approval. Disgraced, she would become an outcast, shunned and exiled from her entire family and Newar community.

Back in Kathmandu, realizing the urgency of the situation and the need to move quickly before the Nepali press broadcast the Rotary team's news in full detail, Aunty frantically formed a plan. She called the Mulepati's circle of close friends—uncles and Rotarians—to an urgent meeting. The group discussed the circumstances, unanimously agreed to support Moni's forbidden marriage to Pem, and came up with a strategy to gain Mohan's approval. No matter what his family friends and son thought, Mohan was the primary family decision-maker and made all decisions about Moni: what school she attended, final choice of husband, whether she could climb, hold a job, etc. Shanti had no say. The uncles figured that once they told Mohan, if they could gently ease the shock by showing their full support of Moni, maybe they could coax him into agreement.

One of the uncles phoned Mohan and called an emergency family meeting without disclosing the subject. As the room filled, Mohan broke into a sweat, worried that something tragic had happened to his daughter while climbing down from the summit. As it turned out, six climbers died on Everest that year.

"I just spoke with her. Did something happen to Moni?" he asked the group, fidgeting nervously.

"No, everything is good with Moni, she's okay," an uncle said, hesitating before speaking again. "Moni and Pem got married at the summit."

A stunned look crossed Mohan's face. The room blurred. In slow motion, he crumpled and fell into his chair and passed out cold. Given Mohan's heart problems and fearing a heart attack, one of the uncles shouted for someone to call a doctor. A few minutes later, Mohan came to, a little woozy and dismayed to find a cluster of people fussing over him.

"*Jita doctor mohh, jita chuyea juu makhu!*" he said, his voice bellowing through the room. "I don't need a doctor. Nothing is wrong with me."

Pushing the chair solidly back underneath him, hands clenched and not looking at anyone in the room, he sat quietly for a moment, the news of his daughter's elopement sinking heavily into the chair with him. One by one, in calm tones, the uncles began speaking, offering a string of reasons for accepting the inter-caste marriage. *Moni summited Everest! She set new world records: first Newari woman to achieve this dangerous and difficult feat. First to be married at Everest's summit. She fulfilled her mission to unfurl the Rotary Nepal Centennial Expedition flag at Everest, putting Nepal on the world stage, invoking national pride. She's famous. What an honorable reflection on the entire Mulepati family!*

Before reaching a decision, Mohan called for Monish, Moni's youngest brother, and told him to come quickly, but not to say a word to his mother. Monish rushed to the meeting and sat down with the group. He had popped a *momo*, a Tibetan dumpling, in his mouth, but stopped chewing the moment his father shared the news. He sat stone sill, a shocked expression on his face.

"Monish, what do you think about this?" Mohan asked.

Monish thought for a second, and with a mouth full of momo, replied, "I agree with the marriage. Pem's a good man and Moni won't be happy with anyone else. They set a record and shouldn't miss this opportunity."

By the end of the meeting, Mohan had agreed to his daughter's marriage and called his wife to break the news. At first, Shanti couldn't speak, then she cried.

"She might have thought that all her dreams were gone by her daughter marrying Pem," Moni said.

Shocked and panicked by the elopement, Shanti immediately called an astrologer to study Moni and Pem's birth charts and horoscopes. To her relief, the match was suitable.

While describing the pain and shock she felt upon learning that Moni had married Pem, Shanti started to cry.

"I felt a deep hurt," she said.

Soni, translating her mother's words, handed her a tissue and put her arms around her shoulders. Mohan, sitting next to his wife, reached over and patted her knee and spoke about her pain. Speaking in English, he explained that what Shanti felt was a family and community pain.

"The gossip and backbiting that we all feared with our daughter marrying outside our caste was a big worry. It's a deep cultural disappointment and shock that lives inside Shanti, a fear, but also a loss of tradition. It took her a long time to recover from her grief."

Traditionally when a daughter marries, she takes the last name and religion of her husband, assuming the dress, prayer, food, and religious celebrations of her husband's family and culture. To a family steeped in the caste tradition, a daughter marrying outside her caste can feel like the loss of a daughter.

Looking back, Mohan acknowledged he was extremely shocked by the news of Moni's marriage to Pem.

"Pem had been in our house, but I had no idea this would happen," he said. "We had been showing Moni photographs of potential husbands and not expecting this. I chose to accept our daughter's marriage, but I didn't know if our community would accept us and our decision."

It was a huge risk for the well-established Mulepati family, but in the end, he trusted his daughter and wished for her happiness.

"How will I live my life if my daughter's not happy?" he said. "If unhappy, you get sick."

While Monish knew Moni and Pem were close, he never suspected they were lovers. Feeling a slight bit of sibling betrayal, he was mad that Moni didn't tell him, but confessed, "Had I known, I probably would have had to tell my parents."

DESCENT

It was approaching noon by the time the team began to descend, right on the edge of their deadline. Pem looked up and noticed a mantle of dark, foreboding clouds forming on the near horizon. He and Kami knew what that meant. Ugly weather was about to blow through. Kami pointed at the sky and said, "Let's go."

Seeing the looks on Kami and Pem's faces, Moni grew nervous. Her first few steps crossing the narrow traverse along the ridgeline seemed even more terrifying than going up. They had to pass ascending climbers on the razor-edge shelf, unclipping and re-clipping into the safety lines as they went around each other. In her journal, she wrote, "I have to get down. God, I was so scared when I looked down. All the other mountains looked so small. If you fall from here, it may be very difficult to find the body."

In bitter cold, the team descended the mountain. Not long into the descent, it started blowing and snowing, making the visibility poor and the route slippery. Their pace was slow. When they reached the Balcony, Pem asked Kami to escort Moni down to Camp IV. He wanted to climb ahead and prepare a reception for Moni. At 6:45 p.m., eight hours after standing on the summit, Kami and Moni arrived at Camp IV, an hour behind Pem. They would have to overnight at 26,000 feet and manage their oxygen supply. They changed their oxygen tanks and wet clothes and, after food and celebration, slept.

That evening, Moni's eyes started to water and burn. When she opened them, the world was black. Terrified, she woke Pem and Kami. Pem held her head and examined her reddened eyes.

"It might be snow blindness," he said, and calmly squeezed eye-drops in both eyes. Earlier that day while climbing down, she had removed her sunglasses when they fogged up in the snow. "Try and sleep," he said.

But Moni worried. They were getting low on oxygen and had a big climb the following day. Her vision might take twenty-four hours or more to clear up, if not longer.

When Moni woke, her eyes were better, but her vision was still reduced to shadowy shapes. Pem was suddenly afraid. *What if I just got married against Moni's family tradition and now Moni is blind?* he ruminated with growing anxiety.

The team packed everything and departed Camp IV at 10:20 a.m., ready to get the climb over with. But first, more troubleshooting. Moni had almost depleted her oxygen supply and they would need a spare. Pem radioed his friend, Lakpa Rita, in search of an extra bottle to purchase. Lakpa Rita's Sherpa was scheduled to bring down unused oxygen tanks from Camp IV and would give them one. Speed Pemba also offered a spare tank. Moni promised to pay them back.

After ten hours of climbing, they finally arrived in Camp II at 7:45 p.m. Both Moni and Pem still felt agitated about how Moni had left things with her family and the tension of limbo. Obsessively, they checked the satellite phone for messages. That evening, they heard back. Her father had approved their marriage, and everyone in her family was happy for them.

The next day, on June 1, at 2 p.m., the team made it safely through the Khumbu Icefall and reached Basecamp. The Sherpas remaining in Basecamp greeted them, looping khadas around their necks and offering congratulations. A wedding cake and a meal of dal bhat awaited them. They took interviews and called home. Pem did not tell his parents that he got married. Communication was a problem as there were no phones in Chyangba village, and since Pem had been independent since the age of twelve, he didn't see the need to make a formal announcement. He would tell his family the next time he was in the village. Besides, one of his aunties knew he was dating a Newar, which meant that the entire village knew. Still, there was a small part of him that was uneasy.

"I was a little worried that my parents would object because I was marrying outside my caste," Pem said.

Back in Bhaktapur, Moni's parents joyfully awaited the arrival of the newlyweds and began arrangements for a traditional Newari wedding ceremony in a temple.

For the moment, Pem's family would have to wait for the news and to meet the bride. In Sherpa tradition, men and women are also expected to marry within their caste, but these traditions are not quite as strict.

"When a man is ready to marry, he will look around the village and find a woman he's interested in, then bring an expensive gift to the family, like beer or whiskey—and ring the doorbell like you were coming for tea," Pem said. "If the family accepts the suitor's offer, they drink to the agreement. If not, the family keeps the gift. Sometimes, when village kids are young, two families will make a toast and promise that their kids will wed when they grow up."

CRASH LANDING

Everest Basecamp, June 2005

Safely back at Basecamp, the team warmed up by the stove and celebrated their victory and received updates on the fate of other expeditions—those that had ended and those still planning to go up. Michiri, they heard, had suffered an asthma attack on the Balcony the day they passed her. Eventually, she surrendered to her Sherpa guide and let him help her down to Basecamp, but the event ended her expedition.

"She was lucky. She almost died," Moni said. "It was like the rabbit and tortoise. She's the rabbit and I'm the tortoise," she added, laughing, her words spoken in the spirit of competitiveness and self-deprecation rather than reprisal.

The team joyfully packed up and waited for a helicopter ride out to Kathmandu. Helicopter services had been busy flying climbers off the mountain for weeks. In the distance, the pulsating thwap of a giant Mi-17 helicopter drew toward Basecamp. Moni, Pem, and Kami stood outside the tented city in a rush of chilly air, staring in the direction of the advancing beat, backpacks in a heap at their feet. The day started benevolently, and they were gaily chattering away, the Nepali prayer flags rippling miles above them in Everest's gusts, their elopement sealed. Moni's snow blindness had diminished, though she still squinted through partially blurred vision. Exhausted from the physical exertion and emotions of summiting, and giddy about their accomplishment, they felt like their lives were cracked open with new possibility.

The inbound helicopter, packed with reporters, would fly them back to Kathmandu, where Pem and Moni would begin their married life. After two grueling months of living in thin air at the cruising altitude of a jet, on a massive, unforgiving glacier of moving ice and rock, the heli-lift seemed like a gift from the gods. The Mi-17 lowered toward the helipad where a giant X had been spray-painted in a sprawling square of stones and well-packed snow. Pem, Moni, and Kami lifted their climbing packs from the ground and moved them closer to the helipad, intending to hop on quickly. Helicopters don't stop long at 17,500 feet.

The Mi-17, nicknamed the *flying tank* by soldiers because of its most reliable and survivable qualities—it can navigate without fuss, and an operational ceiling of 20,000 feet keeps it beyond the range of small arms fire—runs *hot and high* in conditions like Everest. Soldiers are partial to the helicopter's dependable, thick-skinned, armored beast and its conveyance power; it carries thirty-six heavily armed troops or thirty-seven passengers; and four tons of cargo—the equivalent of 3,300 pounds of bombs, rockets, and guns—or twelve stretchers when employed as an ambulance. The Russian-designed military transport helicopter is used primarily in counterterrorism and narcotics, search and rescue, and passenger-cargo transport operations. NATO's code for the Mi-17 is *HIP*. It's a favorite of special ops forces, even though there is nothing stealthy about it.

Moni was walking ahead of the others and noticed that something looked off about the helicopter. She turned to Pem,

"Something doesn't look right," she said.

Pem looked up and, seeing nothing unusual, joked, "Well, you've never been in a helicopter and wouldn't know what it looks like."

A few seconds later, the helicopter angled in sideways and squared up to the helipad, its landing skids hovering above the X. As it lowered, the noisy rotor blades and downwash overpowered those waiting below, blasting them with ground grit. The pilot, wearing headphones and an oxygen mask, leaned toward the windshield and turned his head right then left, and right again, working the pitch control as he landed. About 50 feet in the air, without warning, the helicopter yawed and lost its center of gravity.

It spun sharply, nose up and tail rotor down, and drifted toward the ground. To those standing in the windblast, the velocity blowing off their hats, a slow awareness began to crowd out the noise and violently disturbed air, replacing it with a jolt of recognition: the helicopter was about to crash.

"Back! Back!" Pem shouted. They all ducked and ran.

Kami, who had been video recording the landing, bolted. "I was so scared. I was trying to save myself. I don't want to die now, I thought."

For a moment, the person guiding the helicopter down to the pad disappeared in the chaos. Then the helicopter jerked violently and smashed to the ground, buckling amidst a screech of twisting metal. The rotor blades exploded, sending debris flying across the pad. Bystanders paused before rushing in to rescue the passengers, partially in shock but also afraid the hunk of metal might explode into flames. The prop, still running after the crash, flew across the helipad. After watching Kami's video, Pem speculated that the helipad, which was made mostly of ice packed around stone, had melted in the late May heat, causing the helicopter to tip backward and lose control when it landed on the destabilized pad.

The pilot, dazed but on a mission, cursed at the crumpled cockpit as he crawled out and helped Pem guide the bruised, bleeding, and shaken passengers downhill to safety. A small, wiry reporter, the only one who held onto his camera gear amid the crash and chaos, wanted to conduct an interview with Pem as he moved survivors away from the fray. The reporter's jacket sleeves were torn and covered with black grease and blood that seeped steadily from a narrow gash on his forehead. Despite the danger, the reporter's first imperative—his own personal zenith—was the summit story. He introduced himself and said he was from Nepal Television (NTV), and was overjoyed and impressed that Pem, Moni, and Kami made it to the summit for Nepal and the Rotary Nepal Centennial Everest Expedition. He asked Pem what it was like to marry on the top of the world, and while he was talking, Pem offered his arm and said, "Keep moving."

When everyone had been delivered to safety, Pem, Moni and Kami circled up in the grayish snow, checking for injuries. They dug out extra clothing and sleeping bags from Kami and Moni's backpacks and wrapped them around the injured. Pem's backpack was useless, shredded by the helicopter blades. Moni broke out the expedition camp stove, melted a pan of snow, and brewed a pot of tea. The fresh scent of jasmine and ginger rose in the chaotic air.

A few hours later, after the scene had cleared out and the helipad was rebuilt, the next group of climbers were flown back to Kathmandu, including the Rotary team.

Back in Kathmandu, the Mulepati family hosted a more formal Hindu wedding reception with 200 guests, prayer ceremonies, dinners, dancing, and traditional clothing. Traditionally, newly married couples go live in the groom's family home, but Chyangba was too remote for Pem and Moni's modern taste and career aspirations. For the short term, the couple would live with Moni's parents until they settled into a home of their own.

PART IV

IMMIGRATION:
THE PATH TO US CITIZENSHIP

Nepal.
Hope.
Family.
Duty.
Survival.
A Heap of Red Tape.
America

"We are nothing but we always climb. If you summit and succeed because of your limelight, we will be highlighted, too. And that was true. I always remember this. Sherpas climb all the time, and it doesn't matter —you have to do something special from others— break a record, become popular. Me being a woman, but also marrying at the top was a big highlight."

– Moni Mulepati

THE REACHES OF FAME

By the time the press died down around Pem and Moni's Everest wedding, they were minor celebrities in Nepal. It seemed their star had ascended. Fame would begin to shape their lives in unforeseen ways.

After their Kathmandu wedding, Pem, Moni, and Kami prepared for the promised trip to the Rotary International's 2005 Centennial Convention in Chicago, a reward for their successful expedition and a celebration of Rotary Nepal's pride and new world prominence.

For its 100th anniversary, Rotary International was hosting a big bash, a hoopla that included a black-tie ball, a parade of floats, 43,000 Rotarian attendees and delegates from 153 countries, and a multitude of speakers including messages from Mayor Daley, President Bush, Ted Turner, UN Secretary General Kofi Annan, and Kenyan Nobel Peace Prize Laureate Wangari Maathai. A special ceremony was planned to present the Nepal International Rotary banner that Pem, Moni, and Kami had unfurled at the summit.

For Pem, the trip was an opportunity to move toward his dream of creating a flourishing life in the US—a life not driven by poverty and dismal work opportunities in Nepal. However, in a disappointing turn of events, Rotary Nepal cancelled the team's Chicago trip, ostensibly due to budgetary woes. Only the committee president would attend as a representative and wave the Nepali summit flag. With that devastating news and an open question as to whether they would get another chance like this to drastically alter their life trajectory, Pem feared his dreams and ambitions might slip away. But as is Pem's way, he held out hope. As it turned out, the cancelled trip was a temporary setback. Whatever politics or funding issues at play were erased by Nepal's Finance Minister, Dr. Roop Jyoti, who stepped in and secured plane tickets for Pem, Moni, and Kami, expedited visas, and gave them each $500 cash for travel expenses. Without his help, they might not have made it to America, Moni said, expressing deep gratitude for his generosity and the opportunity. And that was it. The Rotary Nepal Centennial Everest Expedition team flew to Chicago.

When they arrived in the US, their designated contact for an airport pick up was a no-show, leaving the three Nepali climbers befuddled in a crowded Chicago airport. They found a payphone and huddled around the shiny stainless box with its coin slot and return chute, push button numbers, and awkward receiver cradle. While staring at the small print English instructions, they caught the attention of a passerby, who asked if they needed help.

"He told us we had to use coins in the pay phone," Pem recalled. "He gave us some quarters because we didn't have coins, then showed us how to use the phone."

Their designated contact did not answer, so Pem walked over to an airport counter and asked the clerk for the number of the Hyatt hotel where they were booked.

"The man was very rude," Pem reported when he returned to where Moni and Kami waited, his inquiry having failed to produce results. Moni gave her new husband a questioning look. "The man told me, there are so many Hyatts!" he said, shrugging and throwing his hands up in the air.

"Let me go talk to him," Moni said. She approached the man, "Excuse me, we got lost. We are supposed to be at the Hyatt tomorrow. We climbed Everest, can you please help us? It's our first time here."

"Which Hyatt?" the clerk questioned. "There are four just in this area," he said with a prolonged sigh, turning back to his computer screen.

"I know," Moni said politely. "But in Nepal, there is only one!"

She gave the clerk her name and he reluctantly called nearby Hyatts and located their reservation.

"Our first step in America was not good," Moni said, frowning and wagging a finger as she recalled the 2005 experience.

> It was a forty-dollar taxi ride to the Hyatt! When we asked for our reservation, they said we need to pay with a credit card or cash. When I asked how much the room was, they said $250 per room! We had only $500 each. I was ready to go home, but Pem said we should sleep today and tomorrow ask our American friends for help. We were so hungry. They had juices and beer in the fridge, but we didn't eat. Next morning, we got a $200 bill under the door!

Half-starved, the three left the hotel and walked the streets of Evanston, where they discovered a Subway restaurant and split a pricey, foot-long sandwich three ways while discussing how crazy expensive Chicago was. Moni was still hungry and later, in their hotel room, cooked the ramen noodles she had packed in her suitcase before leaving Kathmandu. Meanwhile, Pem called everyone he knew in the US from his trekking business to ask for advice. The next day, to his shock and disbelief, he received a $185 Hyatt phone bill.

"We didn't have the money to pay it!" Pem said, laughing about it now.

Their long-awaited inaugural trip to America was turning out to be not so welcoming. At that point, concerned about the bills stacking up, they needed to decide whether to stay or return to Nepal. Pem, Moni, and Kami went to the convention center and found the Rotary office. A Nepali gentleman told them to stay in their hotel room for the day while he investigated.

"Who will pay?" Moni asked.

The Rotary president's assistant found them and took them to the registration area and told them that they were responsible for all the costs of attending.

"No," Moni replied angrily. "We are going back to Nepal."

The assistant walked them to the President's office. When the secretary asked how their visit was going, Moni assertively, in full detail, spelled out the problems. Pem and Kami stood quietly beside Moni. Apparently, there had been some mistake. The Nepal Rotary team's bill was covered by the Rotary.

"Go eat," she said.

Despite the inhospitable welcome, they stayed and enjoyed the Chicago Convention, taking the stage with the Rotary president to present the Nepal International Rotary banner they unfurled at the top of Everest.

After the convention, they flew back to Kathmandu, where, over the next few months, Pem worked diligently on his Nepal trekking business and a plan to return to the US with his eye on citizenship. Little did he know that the naturalization process would turn out to be nearly as arduous and impossible as summiting Everest.

THE PATH TO CITIZENSHIP

In the fall of 2005, after returning from Chicago to Kathmandu, Pem, and Moni received an invitation from Narayan Shrestha, a Boulder Colorado businessman and Rotarian, to speak at Rotary Clubs across the US with engagements in Colorado, Nebraska, Texas, and Boston. They obtained a tourist visa that allowed them to stay in the US for six months. Over the course of their Rotary addresses, Pem and Narayan raised over $20,000 to build a hydroelectric project in Pem's home village of Chyangba, bringing electricity to the village for the first time—the first of many projects Pem would initiate for his village. Years later, he would help raise $48,000 to bring smokeless stoves to his village, build a school and rebuild it two years later when an earthquake destroyed the buildings, and bring a hospital to the region.

While in Boulder, Pem met Mat Matson, a sixty-nine-year-old Colorado Rotary member who was about to embark on a trek across the entire Continental Divide Trail, or CDT, a wilderness trail stretching 3,100 miles between the US border with Mexico at the trail's southern terminus and Canada to the north. His goal for the Rotary Continental Divide Challenge was to raise $3.1 million to complete the trail and create an endowment for a Rotary-sponsored youth corps trail crew to maintain the Colorado section of the CDT. Mat planned to hike the 3,100 miles one section at a time over a period of four years with a support team. On April 26, 2007, his trek would begin with the 735-mile-long section in New Mexico. In 2008, he and his support team would hike through Colorado, in 2009 Wyoming, and then in 2010 they would complete the trail by hiking through Idaho and Montana, ending at Waterton Lakes National Park inside the Canadian border. A trek like this requires well-thought-out resupply locations and must be timed to avoid winter weather conditions in Colorado's San Juan mountains and the Rocky Mountains on the border of Montana and Canada. Forest fires could alter the schedule at any given time.

Drawn in by Pem's incredible story, his gentle kindness, and the philanthropic work he was doing in Chyangba Village, Mat hired Pem as a guide for the CDT trek and offered to help him work toward US citizenship. Mat had a friend in Boulder who was an immigration lawyer.

Lisa Batten, a third-generation Colorado native, dancer, artist, and immigration lawyer, agreed to take Pem's case. In her practice, she had helped many dancers, artists, and athletes obtain green cards. Colorado is a bit of a hotspot for immigration law given the state-of-the-art athletic training facilities in Colorado Springs and the large number of national, ground-breaking scientific research labs like NOAA, the National Oceanic and Atmospheric Administration; NCAR, the National Center for Atmospheric Research; NIST, among others.

The steps toward US citizenship were daunting, expensive, and, in his case, particularly challenging, Lisa told Pem. But she believed a strong case could be made for an EB-1 visa, an employment-based visa process for foreign nationals with extraordinary ability in the sciences, arts, education, business, or athletics.

For Kami Sherpa, the process was simpler and less expensive. As a Nepali journalist, his petition for political asylum was granted swiftly. The Maoist insurgency, an armed rebellion between the Government of Nepal and the Maoist Communist Party of Nepal that began in 1996 and lasted ten years, had escalated into a full-blown humanitarian crisis. In 2001 and 2005, the Nepali government declared a state of emergency. By the end of the war, brutal assaults had left more than 17,000 civilians, soldiers, insurgents, and police officers dead. Nearly half a million people throughout rural Nepal were uprooted and village governments were displaced, leaving Nepal's economy in shambles.

But Pem didn't meet the qualifications for political asylum and his best chance was an EB-1 visa. With Moni's blessing, Pem began working with Lisa in the hopes of fulfilling his dream to become a US citizen. Lisa began Pem's application for an Extraordinary Ability Visa for Athletes in alpine climbing.

To meet the requirements of an EB-1 visa, a petitioning athlete must meet three out of ten possible criteria. First, Pem had to meet the "extraordinary ability" criteria which, in lay terms, means that you are one of the very few at the top of your field; someone of national or international renown. To demonstrate this in alpine climbing is more problematic than most sports because climbing has no formal ranking systems, national or international championships, world records, Olympic medals, Super Bowls, PGA tours or majors, or a Hall of Fame. Proof of extraordinary ability, a one-time achievement with international claim, would have to be built from more subjective evidence. To meet the two other criteria, Pem would have to demonstrate that he was seeking entry in the same field and would make a future contribution to the United States. Once he became a green card holder, he would have to reside in the US for at least five years before he could become a naturalized US citizen.

The Continental Divide Trail guiding job would help secure Pem's US visa, but the timing was terrible. He and Moni had been living in Colorado in various homes and trailers, relying on friends, when Moni became pregnant with their first child. She was due in April 2007, about the time Pem was scheduled to start his job with Mat on the CDT. The couple discussed their options and agreed that Pem had to go to work. Just two days after the birth their daughter, Pelzom, while Moni was still in the hospital recuperating from a cesarean birth, Pem packed his bags, kissed Moni and his newborn daughter goodbye, and left for the border of Mexico.

Even today, when Moni shares that story, she is always surprised when people ask how she could tolerate being left in the hospital in a foreign country, alone for several months, with a two-day old baby and without the support of her husband, family, or friends. Her response is always the same: "I feel like I can do anything after summiting Everest." As a couple, they were strong, independent, and committed to doing what was necessary to gain US citizenship, determined to beat the obstacles and odds just as they did when summiting Mount Everest.

Even now, when Pem makes trips to Nepal for his trekking business and buying for the store, Moni takes care of the kids, the household, and all their businesses. She uses parts of their climbing story to encourage their two girls—they have two now, Pelzom and Mezel—to push through their own challenges.

"I tell my girls there are lots of ups and downs in life and you must believe you'll get past the storm. You'll feel stronger, more confident. After every night, the sun will come."

In 2010, Pem and Mat finished the Continental Divide trek successfully and on schedule. A year later, the US went into a deep recession. Unable to find a job in Colorado, Pem moved his family to Ann Arbor, Michigan, where he found work with his friend, Heather O'Neal, whom he met in Nepal during his teahouse porter job. Heather ran The Himalayan Bazaar, a business importing Nepali products, and operated a travel agency that led guided tours of Nepal. Pem became the Nepalese product buyer for the store and led trekking trips in Nepal twice a year.

Once Pem secured his green card, with Lisa's guidance, he began the daunting process of gathering documents for the N-400 naturalization application.

"The journey to become a US citizen was even a greater challenge than climbing Everest," he said.

The barriers to acquiring US naturalization are significant. It's a costly administrative nightmare requiring mounds of paperwork and an uninterrupted physical presence in the US. The paperwork included the N400 Application for naturalization plus a massive number of related documents: a declaration of intention to become a US citizen, eligibility documentation, bank accounts, tax returns and affidavits of financial means to support himself and his family, leases, mortgages, birth certificates, his green card, character witnesses, marriage certificate, Nepal passport, biometric finger prints for background checks, photographs, signatures, medical and vaccination records, health insurance. In addition to an English language test and a US civics test, Pem had to pass citizenship interviews, draw money orders, provide self-addressed prepaid envelopes, and submit forms to relinquish his Nepal citizenship. Once documentation is submitted, the wait for a response is long. The process is so onerous that many applicants either give up somewhere in the process or don't bother to apply.

After years of anticipation, applicants receive either a congratulations letter from the White House or a form letter from the department of Homeland Security stamped in big red letters: DENIED. In the latter case, the applicant remains an alien. Reasons: *You have not mastered English. You broke your six-month US residence, didn't file a tax return, failed to demonstrate good moral character. You have poor knowledge of US civics based on incorrect answers given to: who does a US Senator represent? Who is called the Father of Our Country? Who lived in America before the Europeans arrived? What did the Emancipation Proclamation do? Name one US territory.*

It took Pem three months to gather all the paperwork, $22,000, and over nine years of waiting to receive a determination on his citizenship application.

Then, one day, out of the blue, an official-looking envelope arrived in his mailbox.

THE WHITE HOUSE

WASHINGTON

Dear Fellow American:

I am honored to congratulate you on becoming a citizen of the United States of America. You represent the promise of the American Dream, and because of your determination, this great Nation is now your Nation.

You have sworn a solemn oath to this country, and you share in its privileges and responsibilities. Our democratic principles and liberties are yours to uphold through active and engaged participation. I encourage you to be involved in your community and to promote the values that guide us as Americans: hard work and honesty, courage and fair play, tolerance and curiosity, loyalty and patriotism.

Since our founding, generations of immigrants have come to this country full of hope for a brighter future, and they have made sacrifices in order to pass that legacy on to their children and grandchildren. This is the price and the promise of citizenship. You are now part of this precious history, and you serve as an inspiration to those who will come after you.

We embrace you as a new citizen of our land, and we welcome you to the American family.

Sincerely,

Dear Fellow American:

I am honored to congratulate you on becoming a citizen of the United States of America. You represent the promise of the American Dream, and because of your determination, this great Nation is now your Nation.

You have sworn a solemn oath to this country, and you share in its privileges and responsibilities. Our democratic principles and liberties are yours to uphold through active and engaged participation. I encourage you to be involved in your community and to promote the values that guide us as Americans: hard work and honesty, courage and fair play, tolerance and curiosity, loyalty and patriotism.

Since our founding, generations of immigrants have come to this country full of hope for a brighter future, and they have made sacrifices in order to pass that legacy on to their children and grandchildren. This is the price and the promise of citizenship. You are now part of this precious history, and you serve as an inspiration to those who will come after you.

We embrace you as a new citizen of our land, and we welcome you to the American family.

Sincerely, Barack Obama

On April 24, 2015, Pem was granted citizenship. He proudly keeps the mountain of paperwork in a neatly organized and bound, twelve-inch stack on his desk, including the welcome letter from President Obama.

"I feel lucky," Pem admits. "I know many Nepalis who spent $100,000 and never got citizenship. I am blessed and so proud to say I am a US citizen."

He still gets goosebumps when he thinks about this blessing and the happiness and abundance he's experienced with his family here in the US.

"Nepal is still a poor country," Pem said. "It's hard for my friends and siblings who are college educated to find a job. You can't feed yourself or family in one day's work in Nepal."

At first, Moni was more reluctant to give up her Nepali citizenship. She missed her family in Kathmandu, and, unlike her husband, it hadn't been her dream to immigrate to the States. Ultimately, it would be less complicated to travel with Pem and their two girls if she became a US citizen. Besides, America had grown on her. With the opportunities and freedoms she experienced in the US as a businesswoman, motivational speaker, a mother with school-aged girls, a wife whose husband was also her business partner, and quality medical care, she no longer envisioned herself returning to Nepal to live and work. In 2017, two years after Pem, Moni was conferred US citizenship.

Eventually, the couple settled in Ann Arbor, Michigan. On the outskirts of town, they built a beautiful home and life with their two girls. With their newly constructed home, there are no Shrindi. Moni runs the Himalayan Bazaar in downtown Ann Arbor, while Pem runs the trekking company, Imperial Expedition. For several years, Pem owned and ran the Everest Sherpa Restaurant, serving dishes from Nepal, Tibet, and India. They have formed a new family cultural identity by blending their Nepali and American traditions in ways that honor their Sherpa and Newari roots and adopted American culture, keeping their girls grounded as much as possible in the values, language, attitudes, and social structures they grew up with and cherish. At home, the family only speaks Nepali, and they cook customary Nepali meals. For special occasions, the girls wear traditional Nepali clothing. Each morning,

Moni observes a puja drawing on both Sherpa Buddhist and Newari Hindu traditions, teaching the girls the rituals of mantras, offering prayers to gods and deities, and reverence toward the Buddha. They teach their girls etiquette, how to treat guests, and respect for their elders in both Nepali and American traditions.

The girls have traveled to Nepal with Pem and Moni and spent time with each of their families in Kathmandu and Chyangba. But Nepal is a challenge for the girls.

"They're totally Americanized!" Pem said, smiling with pride and acceptance.

They honor the rites of passage of Sherpa, Newari, and American cultures, but do not follow some of the harsher Nepali traditions, such as disciplining children with corporal punishment, which, in Nepal, occurs both at home and at school. They do not adhere to the dowry system or the ancient Hindu tradition of chhaupadi, now illegal, but still practiced in many rural and urban areas of Nepal. Instead, under the wings of a strong-knit family, they nurture their girls' essence and talents—Pelzom's shy, bookish nature that matches her dad's, and Mezel's energetic, rebellious, creative energy, like her mom's. Their daughters are valued and will not be commodities such as girl brides, products of an arranged marriage, or child laborers, nor will they need a dowry to win a suitable husband. They will inherit property, establish and run their own businesses, and make an Everest summit bid if they choose. But neither Pem or Moni believe the girls will follow in their footsteps and climb Everest. For that, Moni breathes a huge sigh of relief.

EPILOGUE

SAVING A VILLAGE

Even as Pem cherishes the American life that he and Moni have carefully built, including a strong community in Ann Arbor, as well as a global community, his heart always returns to Chyangba and to other villages where life remains harsh for so many Nepalis.

Since arriving in the States, Pem has devoted a large portion of his time and money to bringing his family and local villagers to a higher standard of living. With the help of Wongchu Sherpa and Mary Grace Wilkus, vice president of the Tsering's Fund, a Nepali based nonprofit, Pem raised money for a hydroelectric power plant to bring water and electricity to his village. Now, his family and villagers have running water, electricity to power cell phones, computers, and iPads expanding their connection with a larger world. He, along with Wongchu Sherpa and other generous donors, helped build a school in Chyangba so children—both girls and boys—wouldn't have to walk hours to get there, and helped rebuild the school after the 2015 earthquake. Pem has helped organizations like the Tsering's Fund raise money to sponsor Nepali girls to attend college, in the hopes of breaking the cycle of poverty, abuse, and child marriages for these bright young women. He's helped rescue and establish programs to help prevent girls from becoming child laborers or being sold into the sex traffic trade, often discovering abused girls in a remote teahouse or village while trekking with clients. He has helped rebuild homes after earthquakes, calling upon all his friends in the US and across the globe to join the effort. After the 2015 earthquake, Pem built his parents a new, two-story home, though for a long time after the earthquake they were afraid to live in the upper level for fear they would die in the next big quake. Now, they occupy the home.

Out of love and duty, and with grace, Pem Dorjee Sherpa supports his family back in Nepal, helping his brothers Phuri and Ngima by employing them in his trekking business and making sure his brothers and sister have an opportunity to get an education. He sends money home for food, clothing, and other necessities, and for things they dream of but could never afford. He gave the land he purchased and the home he built in Chyangba to his sister and her family. He calls Nepal regularly to ask Dawa and Chhoki if they need anything, checking on their well-being. When Dawa answers the phone, father and son are always brief.

"Sabai rāmrō cha. rkō varṣa tapā'īlā'ī bhēṭnē āśā garchu.

"All good here. Hope to see you soon."

Each call, he asks if they need money, and every time his dad says no.

"As long as I'm alive, I'll work myself," Dawa insists.

As soon as her husband's words echo through the phone, Chhoki grabs the phone from her husband and says, "Pem. Pem. Dad not listening. We need money. So and so has a wedding. So and so has gold necklace; we need one. Brother needs this and that…"

Pem chuckles softly as he describes these conversations, a loving smile spread across his face. He gives an eyeroll when he reviews their iPhone bill and sees that his mother has spent too much time on Tik Tok, gently scolding her in their next conversation.

"My mother is very strong. She act like a tiger to win," he says. "And she is a complainer. She's unhappy about what others are doing. My brother Phuri's girlfriend is not working and sleeping too much. She doesn't like the food people cook. 'I ate at all the village houses and didn't like food,' she tells me. My mom is a good cook," Pem says, smiling, offering a mild deflection and defense.

But he grew a little quieter when talking about a childhood memory of his mother's displeasure with him.

"One day when my sister and I went to feed cow, Mom asked, 'Why you feed cow this grain? You should feed other grain.' When my sister went to milk the cow later and accidently kicked bucket over and lost half the milk, my mother grabbed her and beat her body. Split her nose and bruised her face."

It was terrifying, Pem said. As he thought about what might explain his mother's behavior in that very moment, he believed it was not that the family was starving and the milk was critical to their survival—that wasn't true. They had enough food at the time. It was that there would be no milk tea in the morning.

In some ways, it seems as if Pem never left Chyangba, his heart and presence is still so vibrantly alive there. He feels at home in both Chyangba and Ann Arbor. When he returns to his village, he recognizes that even today, in Nepal's more modern world, there is more work to be done. Boys are still privileged over girls. Young girls are still sold into the sex traffic trade; alcoholism, suicide rates, domestic violence, and mental health issues remain high. Suicide and attempted suicide—typically by hanging or poison—are still a stark reality in the lives of many Nepali women. Little help is available to women (and men) in remote villages, as most psychologists and psychiatrists choose to practice in larger cities like Kathmandu. The financial insecurity of being widowed is still prevalent amongst families working around Mount Everest, and the lack of good-paying jobs forces husbands to live and work far away as migrant workers in the oil rich Arab Gulf countries, for example, and most recently and notably on the construction of the Qatari soccer stadium for the 2022 FIFA World Cup.

The cultural belief that women should not inherit property or express themselves independently, but rather submit to the rules of a male authority—first the father, then the husband, and later, the sons—may have lessened to some degree, but persists, creating alienation, depression, and hopelessness.

Over the years, Pem and Moni have never forgotten what Pem went through in childhood, or the ways Nepali children and families still suffer. Both have made a steadfast commitment to ensuring that their lives would not be impoverished or violent, and to do what they can to help their own families back in Nepal.

MINGMAR

Inside the doorway of a run-down Nepali teahouse in the middle of nowhere, in a warm beam of light, a young, round-cheeked girl hovers over a hard-packed dirt floor, her small hands deliberately wrapped around a grass broom. As she sweeps, a baby sways and twists clumsily over her left hip, his tiny fingers clutching the white and black shawl wrapped around his bottom and knotted at her neck.

She is dressed in a short-sleeved red patterned blouse that falls past her hips over stained grey sweatpants that hang loosely and pile up on her toes. An oversized field hat with a pastel band running through the center covers her cropped, jet-black hair, the brim flopping down across her eyebrows.

Behind her, the light shining off the rows of liquor bottles lining the shelves ignites her smooth, dark skin. She is bent over sweeping when she notices the Sherpa standing near the door, his camera pointed right at her. She stops mid-sweep, the grass broom paused and stretched out in front of her, the lopsided baby gripping her hips with his feet, and stares directly into Pem's camera. Her dark eyes are wide in surprise or curiosity, mouth open, her expression half smiling, half bewildered, as if rooted in the servant world she has been sold into, yet aware of another—a child's world—that is brighter, less capricious.

Her name is Mingmar. She is five years old. Sold to the teahouse owner by a relative and forgotten by her family, she is a child laborer at this mountain teahouse in Siganay Village, a remote settlement of Nepal, an isolated place with no roads or services and little connection to the outside world. The region, wholly unknown to tourists, is traversed on foot by a few locals, yak trains, and villagers passing through to market.

The moment Pem laid eyes on Mingmar, he suspected she was being exploited. His instincts and inquiries proved right. A few days later, Pem walked back up to the teahouse from Chyangba Village with an authority and a posse of strong Nepali men to confront the owner, who admitted having paid 375 rupees for her. They took Mingmar back to Kathmandu and placed her in an orphanage, where she attends school and thrives.

It's hard to imagine the life of this five-year-old girl and

the near impossible odds of her being discovered, let alone rescued, her blotted-out childhood restored in some meaningful way. Pem would not let Mingmar be as invisible as he was in Chyangba. Deep in the heart of Mingmar's story lies the spirit of a Sherpa, a gift from Everest.

ACKNOWLEDGMENTS
CORINNE RICHARDSON

Whenever I travel through Nepal, I am always amazed by how happy and friendly Nepalis are despite living with intractable poverty, meager resources, and inequalities, conditions that have made fighting and violence a regular occurrence in village life. I've often wondered what accounts for this striking quality or way of being, whether Nepalis bear a higher sense of meaning in life—a heightened sense of hope, well-being, and faith beyond what other cultures experience? Perhaps it's their strong sense of belonging and connectedness to the universe, or because their days start out with prayer and ritual. A 2020 article in the *Journal of Nepal Medical Association* credits Nepalis' happiness to spiritualism. Cultural anthropologists affirm that idea, citing Buddhism and other theories, such as the history of Sherpas as merchants in the sixteenth-century Trans-Himalayan trade, and, in the early days, the allure of mountaineering, which offered wages that lifted villagers out of poverty and gave them a sense of freedom and accomplishment.

Whatever the forces at play, I have found Nepalis a joy to be around. Nearly everyone I met in Nepal, in the cities and villages, was warm, humble, inspiring, good-natured, and gracious.

I wish to thank Pem and Moni for their trust and their stories, some of which were painful to share, requiring a commendable level of vulnerability. I am grateful to both for putting me up in their home, feeding me delicious momos, and the many hours they put in working alongside me as they ran three businesses and juggled school schedules and travels to Nepal.

I am grateful to have had the opportunity to spend so much time with Pem, Moni, and their families in the villages, towns, and trails of Nepal, and for the time spent with Khumbu region teahouse owners, Sherpa guides, climbers, porters, teachers, photographers, and videographers along Everest's trekking route. Many thanks to Pem for handling the logistics of Nepal accommodations, travel to Chyangba, interviews, and translators, and the many hours he spent translating for me. The teaching experience he set up for me in the Namche elementary school was quite informative, culturally.

It was a special honor to stay with Pem and Moni's families in Chyangba and Kathmandu. I fell in love with Moni's family. They welcomed me into their fold, fed me, and included me in their traditional ceremonies as if I were a family member rather than an inquisitive nuisance with zero Newari language skills. Shanti graciously put up with my fussy eating habits, and Soni masterfully helped translate her mother's words and feelings. Sitting on the patio overlooking their busy neighborhood, listening to Mohan describe his life story and his feelings about Moni's Everest ascent, was a pure delight. A special thank you to Mohan for speaking English and being so engaging and gracious about responding to deeply personal questions.

An enormous thank you to Moni's brother, Monish Mulepati, for his excellent guided trip through Bhaktapur with his expertise in history and architecture, for showing me the most delicious yogurt in the world, and for sharing family stories from day one with such enthusiasm and superb English fluency. His help with nuanced translations was a gift. His love for family runs deep, and he always made time, despite his hectic night owl schedule running a restaurant.

I would not have been able to write this book without the love and support of my partner, Tom Elliott. His optimism, patience, and belief in me kept me steady. I am grateful for his willingness to adventure to Everest Basecamp with Pem Sherpa and me in 2017, for all the fruitful conversations and critical readings during the making of this book, and for discovering HelloFresh meal delivery. Without his steadiness and tether to home, his encouragement to take a break and go for a ski or mountain bike or get to the sea, I might have faltered.

To my family of friends who encouraged me along the way, talked me through the start, the humps, disappointments, and all the questions, always nudging me forward in exactly the right way: Anne Sexton Bryan, Mary Grace Wilkus, Loren Wright, Susan Edsall, Keith and Marissa Stevens, Marilyn Cuthill, Aimee Boulanger, Kimberly Sterrs, Valley Peters, Stacy Richardson-Baxter, Daphne Gillam, Debby and Tim McKenna, Susan Darden, Kate Cook, Eric Ladd, Peter Schmieding, Kittie Bowen, Monika Paris. *Namaste.*

To my friends who offered quiet spaces in which to write, think, or restore, and skied the trees with me, thank you. Your heartfelt generosity astounds me. Mary Grace Wilkus and Thomas Johnston, Bruce and Pamela Miller, Joanne and Bruce

Fournier, Sarah Elliott, Jimmy Hsu, my childhood sisters, Sarah Wills Viega and Jessica Wills Lipscomb, and the late Sherap Jangbu Sherpa at Panorama Lodge in Namche.

I also wish to thank two precious Nepali girls: Dawa Wangmo Tamang and Tashi Futi Sherpa, the most delightful human beings who continue to teach me about the challenges of being young, modern women in Nepal, and for sharing their village lives, families, and stories with me.

I owe deep gratitude to authors Sonya Lea and Susan Futrell for their critical readings of the manuscript, honest feedback, and for believing that this story belongs in the world and that I was the person to write it. I wish to thank Megan Regnerus for applying her editing skills to the manuscript and her deep conversations about writing and life.

I owe thanks to many people who took the time to be interviewed during the writing of this book, both in the US and Nepal. Kami Sherpa, once overcoming his shyness, told dazzling and terrifying stories of his Everest summits, and brought humor to our conversations about the 2005 Rotary expedition. Lhakpa Sherpa was kind enough to meet with Pem and me several times to talk about Pem's employment at his teahouse. I wish to thank Lisa Batten for describing the intricate process of immigration in lay terms.

A special thanks to my mentor, Sonya Lea, and to Dr. Linda Karell, Associate Professor of English at Montana State University, for the important, meaningful conversations about the problems, sensitivities, and responsibilities of writing an ethnic story, the collaborative aspect of writing, and for reminding me that writing is an act of courage.

I am grateful to my mentors at the University of Iowa who, in the early years of my writing, helped shape my work through their attention and supportive critiques and teasing out the critical threads and themes that mattered most: Patricia Foster, Tom Simmons, and visiting writer Linda Hasselstrom. While at the University of Iowa, I was inspired by the teachings and literary works of Marilyn Robinson, Terry Tempest Williams, and poets Jorie Graham, Jim Galvin, Mark Doty, and Mary Szybist, who generously shared their knowledge of the art and craft of writing, the sound and power of language, and the unity of human experience.

I would like to thank the kind and astute team at DartFrog Books for their expertise, guidance, and insights, and their commitment to bringing this book to print.

Finally, thank you to all my friends and family members for putting up with my prolonged absences while I wrote this book.

Regarding descriptions of Buddhist, Sherpa, Newari, and Hindu beliefs and traditions, inaccuracies might appear between historical versions of Hindu and Buddhist traditions. For this book, it felt important that the point of view, beliefs, and traditions presented should be from the experiences and memories of Pem, Moni, and their families, rather than an academic or historical presentation of Hinduism and Buddhism. Across Nepal, people from many ethnic and religious origins worship common deities in different ways, and it is common to find a blending of religious ideas and traditions, each of which may be personalized and different from its origin. In this book, I relied on Pem and Moni's recounted personal experiences, childhood memories, and their own interpretations of their belief systems and traditions as they practiced them, individually and with their families, in Chyangba and Bhaktapur. I also relied on their families' explanations of local and regional beliefs, traditions, and personal practices as translated to me by Pem and Moni.

ACKNOWLEDGMENTS
PEM SHERPA AND MONI
MULEPATI

We wish to thank everyone who helped us achieve our dreams. We couldn't have done it without the support of so many people and groups. First, we thank our parents Dawa and Chhoki Sherpa, Mohan and Shanti Mulepati, and all our respective family members.

We are grateful to the many people who supported our dreams by helping us get to Everest and the United States, by offering jobs, a place to stay, help with establishing our businesses, and generously donating time and resources to improve the quality of life in Nepali villages. Contributions to Chyangba Village projects, including the installation of smokeless stoves, a hydropower station, a school and hospital, a clean drinking water system, the earthquake rebuild project after the devastating 2015 earthquake, and the funding of a girl's education and leadership program, has made a huge difference in the lives of Nepali people. Dhanyanbad धन्यवाद. Subhāy सुभाय्. Thank you.

Tom Elliott, Gena Fine, Roop Jyoti, Gerri and Greg Kier, Eric and Kaley Ladd, Larry and Pamela Meek, Audrey Matson and the late Mat Matson, Monish Mulepati, Heather

O'Neal, Robin and Waddy Potthoff, Rotary International, Rotary Club of New Road City, Rotary Centennial Everest Expedition team, Rotary Club of Port Nicholson, NZ, Peter and Karen Schmieding, Kami Sherpa, the late Wongchu Sherpa, Narayan and Sreejana Shrestha, Ambika Shrestha, Philip Toohey, Mary Grace Wilkus and Thomas Johnston, Peter and Barbara Wittington.

A sweet dedication to our beloved daughters Pelzom & Mezel.

We would like to honor three important people in memoriam: Colorado Rotary member Mat Matson, Wongchu Sherpa, and mountaineer and filmmaker David Breashears. David made a significant contribution to promoting climbing and tourism in Nepal. His passing is a big loss for the mountaineering community around the world. We are grateful for the time we had with him.

Mat Matson, the Rotary district governor from Conifer, Colorado, gave me the job that opened the door to becoming a US citizen. We are deeply grateful for Mat's invaluable help in becoming a US citizen and the great memory of hiking the Continental Divide Trail.

Wongchu Sherpa owned a large expedition company. He led people to the highest mountains and provided jobs for many in our village, including me. Wongchu cared deeply about tourism in Nepal and improving the quality of life in our village. He loved the mountains and inspired many adventurers. His passing is a significant loss for our village and the tourism industry in Nepal.

Lastly, a special thanks to Corinne Richardson, who was willing to dedicate her time and energy to share our stories with the world. Corinne's support and dedication has played an invaluable role in bringing our vision to life. She is responsible for picking up the best moments of our life and putting them down on paper in words for the world to read. We hope they are inspirational to readers.

With love and gratitude,
Moni and Pem Sherpa

RESOURCES

Regarding the history, geography, economics, politics, and culture of Nepal, and the Everest Mountaineering culture, the following sources were invaluable as I was researching and writing this book:

Douglas, Ed. 2021. Himalaya: A Human History. New York: W.W. Norton & Company.

Ortner, Sherry B. 1999. Life and Death on Mt. Everest: Sherpas and Himalayan Mountaineering. Princeton, NJ: Princeton University Press.

Poudel, Anita. 2020. "Role of Spirituality in Mental Health in Nepal." Journal of Nepal Medical Association 58 (226): 439–441. https://doi.org/10.31729/jnma.5110.

Journalist Elizabeth Hawley's chronicles of Everest climbing expeditions compiled in the *Himalayan Database: The Expedition Archives of Elizabeth Hawley*, www.himalayandatabase.com, were extremely useful. Her detailed records spanning from 1905 to 2017—including dates, camps, routes, Sherpas, climbers and their nationalities, summits, deaths, accidents, rescues, and the use of supplemental oxygen—provides a rich historical account of mountaineering's most coveted peak, reflecting a century of changes on Everest.

Respected mountaineer Alan Arnette's website and blog, www.alanarnette.com, offered excellent coverage of Everest expeditions and seasons with photos, videos, podcasts, and human-interest stories, providing a broad, insider's description of mountaineering life and culture on Everest. His route maps, elevations, and climbing distances and times between camps were a great resource.

There is an abundance of interesting scientific and medical information on the effects of oxygen deprivation on the human body at high altitude. I read and drew on the following materials to understand these impacts, especially those specific to Mount Everest, and the reasons some mountaineering Sherpas are not as vulnerable to these effects:

Peacock, A J."ABC of Oxygen: Oxygen at High Altitude." BMJ 317,7165 (1998): 1063-1066. https://doi. org/October 17, 1998.

Sohn, Emily."The Science Behind The Super Abilities Of Sherpas."NPR.May28,2017.https://www.npr.org/ sections/goatsandsoda/2017/05/28/530204187/ the-science-behind-the-super-abilities-of-sherpas.

Details about Delsalle's landing a helicopter on Everest were found in Vertical Mag:

"Landing on Everest: Didier Delsalle Recalls His Record Flight." Vertical Mag. November 2, 2017. https://verticalmag.com/features/landing-everest-didier-delsalle-recalls-record-flight/.

For death statistics on Everest, the following works were consulted:

Altitude Himalaya. "The Everest Death Zone: Unveiling the Mysteries and Dangers at 26,000 Feet. Altitude Himalaya website. https://www.altitudehimalaya. com/blog/everest-death-zone.

Firth, Paul et al. "Mortality on Mount Everest, 1921-2006: Descriptive Study." BMJ 337, no. dec11 1 (December 11, 2008). https://doi.org/10.1136/ bmj.a2654.

Jacobs, Frank. "Mapped: The Deadly Geography of Mount Everest." Big Think, January 31, 2024. https:// bigthink.com/strange-maps/everest-deaths/.

"Nova | Transcripts | Everest: The Death Zone." PBS, February 24, 1998. https://www.pbs.org/wgbh/ nova/transcripts/2506everest.html.

With regard to the geological information on the Khumbu Glacier movement, the following sources were useful:

Altena, Bas, and Andreas Kääb. "Ensemble Matching of Repeat Satellite Images Applied to Measure Fast-Changing Ice Flow, Verified with Mountain Climber Trajectories on Khumbu Icefall, Mount Everest." Journal of Glaciology 66, no. 260 (2020): 905–15. https://doi.org/10.1017/jog.2020.66.

"Copernicus Sentinel-2 monitors glacial icefall, helping climbers ascend Mount Everest." Sentinel Success Stories. September 2020. https://sentinel.esa.

int/web/success-stories/-/copernicus-sentinel-2-monitors-glacier-icefall-helping-climbers-ascend-mount-everest

Starmer, Jack. "Glacial Movements in the Khumbu Icefall." The American Alpine Club. https://publications.americanalpineclub.org/articles/12199511000/Glacial-Movement-in-the-Khumbu-Icefall.

For information on Nepal's poverty and suicide rates, the following sources were consulted:

Bhattarai, Sewa. "Nepal's Suicide Rate Vastly Underestimated." Nepali Times (Patan Dhoka Lalitpur), January 10, 2020. https://nepalitimes.com/here-now/nepal-s-suicide-rate-vastly-underestimated.

Hughes, Kirra L. "Suicide Rates Among Young, Married Women in Nepal." Master's thesis, School for International Training, 2012. https://digitalcollections.sit.edu/capstones/2850/.

World Bank. "At a Glance." The World Bank Group. https://www.worldbank.org/en/country/nepal/overview

Other texts that were inspirational while writing this book include *Caste: The Origins of Our Discontents* by Isabel Wilkerson; *Writing the Other* by Nisi Shawl and Cynthia Ward; and *Whiteness Is Not an Ancestor* by Lisa Iverson, specifically Sonya Lea's essay, *"Bloodlines: A Legal Lynching and a Family's Reckoning."*

To recreate Pasang Rinji's story, I relied on Pem's memories, the recollections of his parents, Dawa and Chhoki, as well as Chyangba Village elders, as told to Pem in Sherpa which he translated to English. I also relied, in part, on my experiences in Chyangba for landscape descriptions. The italics signal a collective voice behind the story's telling, and that some details are speculative or imagined.

Everest photo credits: Pem Dorjee Sherpa, unless otherwise attributed.

ABOUT THE AUTHOR

Corinne Richardson is a graduate of the Nonfiction Writing Program at the University of Iowa and holds an MFA in English. She lives in Montana. *Beyond Everest* is her first book.

Printed in Great Britain
by Amazon